EDUCATION OF THE SCHEDULED CASTE PEOPLE

EDUCATION OF THE SCHEDULED CASTE PEOPLE

Namasudras of West Bengal

N.B. Biswas
N.R. Roy

SHIPRA

ISBN: 978-81-7541-717-5

First Published in India in 2014

Education of the Scheduled Caste People: Namasudras of West Bengal

Published by:
SHIPRA PUBLICATIONS
H.O.: LG 18-19, Pankaj Central Market, Patparganj,
I.P. Ext., Delhi-110092, Tel: 91-11-2223 5152, 2223 6152
Br.Off.: 4617/18, Ansari Road, Darya Ganj,
New Delhi-110002, Tel: 9650028065, 9810522367
E-mail: info@shiprapublications.com
www.shiprapublications.com

Preface

The Scheduled Caste of India constitutes around 16.20 per cent to the total population of the country. This Scheduled Caste groups are very backward in respect to their socio-economic condition, education, political and in others aspect from the very beginning of the Indian history. Almost all the states of the country possess Scheduled Caste population in certain extent. The state West Bengal is not an exception in this regard. The state has around 23 per cent Scheduled Caste population in its total population. But their socio-economic condition, educational aspect and others aspect are very poor in comparison to the other people of the state. The Namasudra is one of the sub-castes of Scheduled Caste population in the state. Their number is very large in comparison to the other sub-caste of Scheduled Caste group in the state. But, so far their educational development is concerned they are backward than the others groups of people as well as general people of the state.

Based on primary as well as secondary data, for which the authors have conducted a survey type research work, the study attempts to find out the participation level of education by the Namasudra people in special and scheduled caste people in general of the state. Again, the researchers have found out the attitudes of Namasudra students, parents and community members regarding the education from the state and attempt has been made to compare their attitudes regarding education within the same group and with other groups, to see how far they have favourable attitudes towards education. So far the socio-economic conditions of the Namasudra in the state are concerned, they are very poor, so, they prefer to send their children to the income generated work to meet economic problem of the family. As a result a big portion of the population remains untouched from education and which create illiteracy problem in the country, even though lot of good schemes have been taken up by the government to abolish illiteracy from the Nation. However, those who are sending their kids to the school they are also facing a number of problems due to which they are unable to continue their study further. So, in the present study the authors explore the various problems faced by the Namasudra students at their secondary level of education and recommend some equitable suggestions for the better participation in education by the said groups in the state.

Contents

I

Educational Scenario of Scheduled Castes of India

Traditionally, the Indian society is based on a caste system with massive inequalities in social, economical and political spheres. The perpetuation of social and economic inequalities further strengthened the division of society along the caste lines wherein the occupation and the status got determined at the time of birth, depending upon the type of family in which one is born and not by the individual initiatives, aptitude, educational attainment or skills acquired during the working life. The potent instrument used to perpetuate the socio-economic differentials was the separation of work from knowledge and power. The working class was denied access to education as it was considered a privilege of few elite groups. The denial of education was essential to prevent them from acquiring rights in productive assets, mainly land, which was in the hand of upper castes who seldom worked on it. On the other hand, the lower castes being without land and other productive assets were forced to seek employment from the land owning class and were at their mercy. This manifested itself in the prevalence of bonded labour, whereby the working class even lost the choice of work place. Many of them got tied to their master because they remained indebted for generations together. Absence of education and lack of awareness forced the lower classes to work as manual labourers, many of them working in unclean occupations like scavenging etc., from one generation to another. Politically, the former due to their higher status yielded more power and the latter were powerless and unorganized.

After the attainment of independence of India, this relationship of master-slave type was sought to be changed as equality of opportunity and social justice were recognized the guiding principles of development planning in independent India. Three types of approaches were followed to overcome the historical malaise. Firstly, abolition of untouchablity and discrimination on the basis of caste, creed and religion to ensure that these provisions are adhered to, constitutional guarantees and a number of legislative provisions have been made. Secondly, equality of access in education was considered as an important aspect of achieving equity and social justice. Therefore, to ensure that economic deprivation does not stand in the way of access to education and other opportunities, a number of measures like friendships, scholarships, incentives and attendance scholarships are provided. Thirdly, an appropriate reservation in the recruitment and promotion to various government and public sector jobs was made mandatory so as to ensure their entry and vertical mobility into organized labour market particularly in non-agricultural occupations.

Despite a variety of provisions, the outcome has been quite mixed. While the government has been extending the provisions of protective discrimination from one decade to another, it is generally felt that some castes have progressed faster to the exclusion of the others thus perpetuating the intra-caste differentials within the scheduled castes. There are many instances when intra-caste disparities and differentials are more pronounced then those prevailing between the scheduled caste and scheduled tribes and others as a whole. The differentials in educational attainment and access to elementary and other levels of educations have also continued to perpetuate. This calls for a detailed examination of the outcomes of educational and other efforts undertaken during the last four decades.

GENESIS OF SCHEDULED CASTE

The word Scheduled Caste presents fuzziness. In a caste based society, they designate a category constituting the lower and depressed section of populace. The term *Depressed* for the first time was used in 1931 census for classification of those who were regarded as outcastes or untouchables and those who suffered from various social disabilities in the matter of education and general and general advancement. They occupied a peculiar position in our social and political system. Socially these castes occupied the lowest tread of the caste hierarchy and were involved in the most debasing jobs and to add insult to injury were considered to pollute those whom they happen to touch even innocently. The expression "Scheduled Caste" was first used by the Simon Commission and embodied in the Government of India Act of 1935. Before 1935 they were known as untouchables of exterior castes or depressed castes. They were in fact, outside the caste (Varna) system. They were external in the sense that they were not allowed to live within the village settlement where people other than these group of people did live. Naturally they lived outside the village settlement. Mahatma Gandhi termed this caste 'Harijans' meaning people of God (Hari means God and Jans means people). They are being deprived socially, economically and politically for generations. In the traditional Indian society the deprivation of one section of people to another gave rise to social inequality. This still persists in our society and economy. The worst victims or sufferers are the scheduled castes are the dalits. The Constitution of India guarantees some of the privileges to this section which are also received by other citizens.

Thus a special category of castes known as 'scheduled castes' was created by the British Government for the purpose of dividing the Hindu population in pursuance of its 'Divide and Rule' policy. They were neither 'untouchables' whose cause was so assiduously championed by Ambedkar, nor the depressed classes as defined by the Lothian Committee, specially constitute for the purpose of defining and enumerating the depressed classes, solely on the criteria of: (a) denial of access to the interior of ordinary Hindu temple, and (b) causing pollution by touch or within a certain distance, but "a group of castes, races or tribes which appear to correspond to the classes of persons formerly known as "depressed classes" as the Majesty in council may specify". Earlier the prevailing idea had been that inclusion in the list of Depressed Classes might affect the social prestige of the castes. The scheduling of castes on the basis of social, political, economic and educational level of development removed that stigma so much so that even those castes which only a decade earlier had asked for exclusion from the list of Depressed classes no longer pressed for it, because of the apparent political, economic and educational benefits. From now on, the process of upward mobility of castes either by the 'Sanskritization' process or by the 'Evangelical' process not only got stalled but actually a reverse process set in, that of inclusion of castes in the list of 'Scheduled Castes' which continues to remain the official designation for untouchables down to the present, though the term was primarily coined to denote those who would enjoy the special electoral arrangements for the 'Depressed Classes' under the 1935 Act.

Criteria for Scheduling

(a) The scheduled castes and the scheduled tribes form a significant part of the Indian social structure, and are economically and socially backward. These communities are referred as 'scheduled' because they have been listed on the basis of special disabilities suffered by them in appropriate schedules for each state or administrative area. They were first listed as such, under the Government of India Act, 1935. The constitution of India also requires the president to list those state wise. The term thus denotes a constitutional classification and not sociological one.

(b) Their social and economic backwardness may be identified on the basis of following grounds—
   (i) They are occupying a lower position in the Indian social structure and the caste hierarchy of Hindu social organization;
   (ii) There is a lack of general educational development among the major sections of these communities;
   (iii) Their representation is inadequate in Government services;
   (iv) They suffer from inadequate representation in the field of trade, commerce and industry;
   (v) They have been suffering from social as well as physical isolation from the other groups.

PRESENT EDUCATIONAL SCENARIO

In an age of information revolution, education the way of imparting and acquiring of knowledge to teaching and learning in the conscious process by which a person learn and applies the learning for his life experiences. Over the time, facilitating and providing education has become one of the most important functions of the state. It is an instrument in awakening in a person, the cultural values, preparing for a better, practical training and helping him to learn and adjust to the surrounding social and natural environment. For the underprivileged section of the society, like the member of scheduled castes in India, who was subjected to deprivation of various forms over countries, education seems to be the most important tool of empowerment. Education has been treated as a fundamental human rights enshrined in the Universal Declaration of the Human rights and the International Human Rights Covenants, achieving the rights for the Basic education particularly for the under privileged sections of the society of these scheduled caste community which is not only the obligation of the state but the biggest moral challenges of our times.

Within the broad spectrum of views on education from the narrow concept of schooling and skill formation to the broad vision of growth and development of a person in life within the society/mentally and spiritually education is a continuous learning process through various stages of the development of a person, as an individual or as group adjustment with the society as at large, earning and spending of the income and participation in civic affairs which involves a whole gamut of issues like general welfare, freedom, appeal to reason and pervading happiness including access and entitlement to equal like of opportunity in imparting education to all but with a forms on the development of less privileged so that they are brought on the same platform with the privileged in matters of employment and developing their skills to get suitable employment. Following the concept of Swami Vivekananda that education is the manifestation of innate qualities of the person the state has a liability to educate its people. Education, therefore, is the most crucial tool of empowering people the primary vehicle by which economically and socially marginalized adults and children can are empowered to lift themselves from the existing levels of poverty and in obtained the means to participate fully in their communities. Unless these underprivileged sections of the society receive the minimum education, they cannot exercise the civil, political, economic and social freedom as preserved in the constitution of India. India, the largest democracy of the world, unfortunately houses the largest number of underprivileged and uneducated persons, who have remained deprived of the heritage of cultural continuity of the country as well as that of the human kind.

Apart from fighting inequality and discrimination meted out to the members of scheduled castes in the tradition bound Indian society the formers of the Constitution have visualized a number of steps by way of "Compensatory Discrimination". Apart from guaranteeing in a number of economic, social and political rights to the members of scheduled castes Article 46 of the constitution, therefore, focuses on the very basic tool of empowering the members of scheduled castes through education and economic rights: "the state shall promote with special care the education and economic interests of the weaker sections of the people, and in particular to the scheduled castes and scheduled tribes, and shall protect them from special injustice and all forms of social exploitation".

Education promotes all round and harmonious development of the nation. It nurtures the potentialities of its members and channelize into appropriate avenues to develop them as effective, productive, efficient and responsible participants in different social roles—instrumental also expressive. It makes the man rational and enables them to perceive and examine things in proper perspective. Education is the most important element in the development of any community. The role of education as an investment in human resources has been increasingly recognized in all countries. For all round development of the Indian society the importance of educational development of general masses is a well-established fact universally accepted. Social and religious reformers in India realized the importance of education and worked for the educational uplift of the people throughout the ages. Education has special significance, particularly for the weaker sections of the society, for whom, education is an input not only for their economic development but also for instilling in them self-confidence and inner strength, thereby enabling them to face the new and unforeseen challenges. The poor progress of the lowest castes, especially those suffering from the disabilities of untouchability, in the traditional Brahmanical Sanskrit education in the pre-British days, was partly due to the strong caste prejudices and prevalence of the practice of untouchability. Steeped in ignorance, illiteracy and poverty, they have been target of economic exploitation, harassment, atrocities and all forms of social disabilities.

The Government has special concern and commitment for the well being of the socially disadvantaged groups like the scheduled castes (SCs), as they still continue to lag behind the rest of the society due to their social and economic backwardness. These groups, which passed through the process of welfare and development during the past four decades, will now be empowered to act as agents of socio-economic change and development. According to the Census data, the percentage of scheduled caste population to the country's total population was 14.82 per cent in 1971, 15.75 per cent in 1981, 16.48 per cent in 1991 and 16.20 (total, 16,66,35,700) percent in 2001. Of the total scheduled caste population, more than 90 per cent live in rural areas; only less than 10 per cent live in urban areas.

Literacy can be defined as the ability to read and write with understanding in any one language. The percentage of literate people out of the total population of the country is known as the literacy rate of that nation. In India literacy rate is 65.38 per cent as per 2001 census. But this rate is not uniform and may vary according to region, religion and gender. Urban literacy rate is much more than rural, male literacy rate is higher than the female literacy rate. The following Table 1.1 illustrates the point:

The above mentioned table shows the progress of education among the Indian peoples since 1901 to 2011. In 1901 the literacy rate was only 5.53 per cent, but in 2011 the literacy rate stood up to 74.04 per cent. But

Table 1.1: Progress of General Literacy in India from 1901-2011

Census Year	*Total Literacy*
1901	5.53
1911	5.92
1921	7.16
1931	9.5
1951	18.33
1961	28.3
1971	34.45
1981	42.57
1991	52.21
2001	65.38
2011	74.04

Sources: Various Census of India from 1901-2011, RGI.

still this progress is not up to the mark as because, after 66 years of independence we failed to achieve the 100 per cent literacy, though it is the first priority of the Govt. of India.

On the other hand development of education among scheduled caste is slower than the general people. According to the Census of India 2011 the literacy rate in India is 74.04 per cent, whereas scheduled caste literacy rate only 63.89 per cent. The literacy rate among the scheduled castes as per 2001 census was 54.69 per cent, in 1991 it was 37.41, while it was only 21.38 according to 1981 census. It shows that within a decade, literacy rate increased by 19.03 per cent. Scheduled caste literacy rate was highest in Kerala (79.66%), and lowest in Bihar (19.49%). In case of general literacy rate Kerala took the highest position (89.81%) and Bihar's position was the lowest i.e. 38.48 per cent. If we consider the state with relatively higher share of scheduled caste population viz. Punjab, Himachal Pradesh, Uttar Pradesh and West Bengal, we see that in all these states the SC literacy rate more than 40 per cent. In Uttar Pradesh it was 26.58 per cent. The literacy rate of Uttar Pradesh was also very low, but the general literacy rate of the rest three states was higher than the National average.

From the Table 1.1 it is become very clear that the literacy rate of Indian people is growing in mediocre rate of pace.

Development of education among scheduled caste in different state of the country may be better understood from the following census tables.

From the above Table 1.2 that it is found that the scheduled castes people of all the states are not equally developed in the field of education. The state Mizoram having the highest literacy percentage among scheduled caste (98.40%) and lowest literacy rate found in the state Bihar

(37.67%) according to the census 2011 of India. The literacy rate of the state Mizoram, Kerala and Daman and Diu is more than 90 per cent. The literacy rate of the states Uttar Pradesh, Rajasthan, Karnataka, Jharkhand, Bihar and Andhra Pradesh are below than the national level scheduled caste's literacy rate and rest of the states are having better

Table 1.2: State/Sex-Wise Literacy of Scheduled Castes in India 2011

State/UTs	*2001*			**2011*		
	Person	*Male*	*Female*	*Person*	*Male*	*Female*
Andhra Pradesh	53.52	63.51	43.35	62.72	72.71	52.55
Arunachal Pradesh	67.64	76.31	54.99	76.84	85.51	64.19
Assam	66.78	75.74	57.14	75.98	84.94	66.34
Bihar	28.47	40.23	15.58	37.67	49.43	24.78
Chhattisgarh	63.96	78.70	49.22	73.16	87.79	58.42
Goa	71.92	81.56	62.05	81.12	90.76	71.25
Gujarat	70.50	82.56	57.58	79.70	91.76	66.78
Haryana	55.45	66.93	42.26	64.65	76.13	51.46
Himachal Pradesh	70.31	80.01	60.35	79.51	89.21	69.55
Jammu and Kashmir	59.03	69.57	47.46	68.23	78.77	56.66
Jharkhand	37.56	51.59	22.55	46.76	60.79	31.75
Karnataka	52.87	63.75	41.72	62.07	72.95	50.92
Kerala	82.66	88.07	77.56	91.86	97.27	86.76
Madhya Pradesh	58.57	72.33	43.28	67.77	81.53	52.48
Maharashtra	71.90	83.29	59.98	81.10	92.49	69.18
Manipur	72.32	81.78	62.97	81.52	90.98	72.17
Meghalaya	56.27	65.86	45.21	65.47	75.06	54.41
Mizoram	89.20	88.44	92.16	98.40	97.64	100
Nagaland	–	–	–	–	–	–
Orissa	55.53	70.47	40.33	64.73	79.67	49.53
Punjab	56.22	63.38	48.25	65.42	72.58	57.45
Rajasthan	52.24	68.99	33.87	61.44	78.19	43.77
Sikkim	63.04	70.15	55.71	72.24	79.35	64.91
Tamil Nadu	63.19	73.41	53.01	72.39	82.61	62.21
Tripura	74.68	81.85	67.24	83.88	91.05	76.44
Uttar Pradesh	46.27	60.34	30.50	55.47	69.54	39.70
Uttaranchal	63.40	77.26	48.74	72.60	86.46	57.94
West Bengal	59.04	70.54	46.90	68.24	79.74	56.10
Andaman and Nicobar Islands	–	–	–	–	–	–
Chandigarh	67.66	76.20	57.22	76.86	85.40	66.42
Dadra and Nagar Haveli	78.25	88.37	67.05	87.45	97.57	76.25
Daman and Diu	85.13	94.03	75.82	94.25	100	85.02
Delhi	70.85	80.77	59.07	80.05	89.97	68.27
Lakshadweep	–	–	–	–	–	–
Pondicherry	69.12	78.41	60.05	78.32	87.61	69.25
India	54.69	66.64	41.90	63.89	75.84	51.10

*Projected data.

Source: Census of India 2001, RGI.

literacy rate than the national level scheduled caste literacy rate. In every year literacy percentage of the scheduled caste people are improving day by day, but still they are lagging behind in their social setting. If we compare the literacy among the general population of India, than it is found that the progress of education is slow than the general literacy of the country. The following Table 1.3 shows the literacy rate of general people and scheduled caste people's literacy progress from 1961-2011.

Table 1.3: Progress of Scheduled Caste's Literacy in India from 1961-2011

Census Year	*Scheduled Caste*	*General*
1961	10.27	28.3
1971	14.67	34.45
1981	21.38	42.57
1991	37.41	52.21
2001	54.69	65.38
2011	*63.89	74.04

Source: Various Census of India from 1961-2011.*Projected data.

From the table it is found that the literacy rate of Scheduled Caste in the country is very poor in comparison to the national level general people's literacy rate in all the censuses reports. It is revealed from the above table that according to the census 1961 the scheduled caste literacy rate was 10.27 per cent, whereas the general people's literacy rate was 28.3 per cent which is more than the double. Again in the census 2011 the SCs literacy rate is 63.89 per cent, but the general people's literacy rate is 74.04 per cent. This comparative development of education among scheduled caste and general people in India may be shown through the following graph also.

From the histogram (Fig. 1.1) it is very clear that the growth rate of participation in education among scheduled caste is lower than the general people of India in various years of censuses.

EDUCATIONAL SCENARIO OF SCHECULED CASTES OF WEST BENGAL

One of the important indicators for development is education, especially for the backward people like Scheduled Castes and Scheduled Tribes. Since this section of our society has always been backward and deprived of basic rights, education has largely been far from their reach. Although our country could not come out from the darkness of illiteracy after the 65 years of independence, the socio-economic development of the

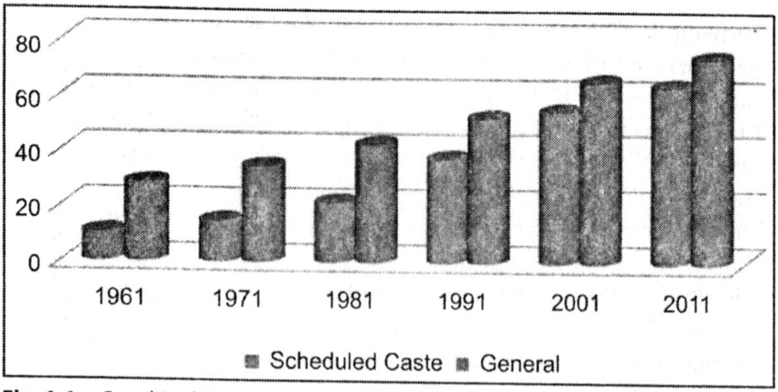

Fig. 1.1: Graphical Representation of Comparative Growth of Scheduled Caste and General Literacy in India from 1961-2011

Scheduled Caste and their integration with the mainstream is constitutional responsibility and a national goal. Achieving of this noble demand effective planning and implementation of the programme for the development of the Scheduled castes is required.

The Scheduled Castes in West Bengal cover about 23.00 per cent (1,84,52,555) according to the Census 2001 of India to the population of the state. In 1981 they shared 21.99 per cent and in 1991, 23.62 per cent to the total population of the state.

The percentage of literates among the scheduled castes of West Bengal 2011 census is 68.24 per cent, whereas the said percentages were 59.04 per cent in 2001, 42.21 per cent in 1991, 24.42 per cent in 1981, 17.80 per cent in 1971 and 13.58 per cent in 1961.

The percentage of scheduled caste of different districts of West Bengal varies from census to census. There are eighteen (18) districts in West Bengal, and where large numbers of scheduled caste are living; but their development in the field of education varies from district to district.

Out of eighteen districts North 24 Paragana, Kolkata and Koch Bihar possess highest literacy rate such as—79.99 per cent, 79.74 per cent and 75.50 per cent respectively according to the census 2011; and lowest literacy rate possess the districts like—Banker, Puruliya and Birbhum with the percentage 52.12 per cent, 54.35 per cent and 54.94 per cent respectively. In 2001 also the following districts such as—North 24 Paragana, Kolkata and Koch Bihar possess highest literacy rate such as—70.79 per cent, 70.54 per cent and 66.30 per cent respectively; and lowest literacy rate possess the districts like—Banker, Puruliya and

Birbhum with the percentage 42.92 per cent, 45.15 per cent and 45.74 per cent respectively. Again in the census 1991 the districts possess highest literacy rate was Kolkata, Medinipur and North 24 Paragana with the literacy rate—56.53 per cent, 54.56 per cent and 53.51 per cent respectively; and lowest literacy rate was found in the districts Birbhum, Banker and Puruliya with the literacy rate 27.66 per cent, 29.96 per cent and 31.81 per cent respectively. From the report it is found that the districts Banker, Birbhum and Puruliya could not achieve much in the field of education by the scheduled caste population in both the census period. It is also found from the various reports that out of 18 districts nine (9) districts lies above the measuring line, these districts are—Koch Bihar, Jalpaiguri, Kolkata, North 24 Paragana, South 24 Paragana, Darjeeling, Naida, Haora and Medinapur; and rest of the districts are lying the below measuring line.

The Table 1.4 shows the lliteracy Rate of Scheduled Castes in West Bengal of different Districts from 1961-2011.

Table 1.4: Literacy Rate of Scheduled Castes in West Bengal of Different Districts from 1961-2011

Sl. No.	*State/Districts*	*1961*	*1971*	*1981*	*1991*	*2001*	**2011*
1.	West Bengal	13.58	17.80	24.42	42.21	59.04	68.24
2.	Koch Bihar	17.18	18.28	25.21	41.07	66.30	75.50
3.	Jalpaiguri	9.77	16.86	23.05	41.34	61.87	71.07
4.	Darjeeling	22.24	24.71	31.77	46.30	62.43	71.63
5.	Uttar Dinajpur	10.84	15.91	20.03	33.05	50.06	59.26
6.	Daxin Dinajpur	–	–	–	–	54.55	63.75
7.	Maldah	10.51	13.49	20.41	33.89	51.17	60.37
8.	Murshidabad	8.81	11.47	17.07	32.79	48.91	58.11
9.	Nadia	16.76	21.27	27.51	45.32	63.09	72.29
10.	North 24 Paragana	19.01	26.08	33.28	53.51	70.79	79.99
11.	South 24 Paragana	–	–	–	49.79	59.01	68.31
12.	Kolkata	28.07	31.64	42.59	56.53	70.54	79.74
13.	Haora	16.22	25.67	28.80	44.87	61.13	70.33
14.	Hugli	11.80	13.21	22.50	40.66	56.10	65.30
15.	Medinipur	14.90	19.50	26.76	54.56	63.57	72.77
16.	Banker	7.20	10.09	14.93	29.96	42.92	52.12
17.	Puruliya	7.05	10.41	18.46	31.81	45.15	54.35
18.	Burdhwan	9.77	11.35	15.79	36.57	51.99	61.19
19.	Birbhum	7.32	10.13	14.79	27.66	45.74	54.94

*Projected data.

Source: Census reports of India, RGI, 1961-2001.

In the state West Bengal as we have found that, there are fifty nine (59) sub-communities among the scheduled caste people. Out of these fifty nine only few groups are very successful in the field education and majority scheduled castes groups remain unsuccessful. According to the census 2011, the following sub-communities of scheduled castes are having highest literacy rate among the others sub groups, they are—Konowr (92.15%), Sunri (91.48%), Dhoba, Dhubi (83.13%), Kandra (81.35%), Pod, Poundra (81.30%), Namasudra (81.13%), Damai (79.03%), Kadar (78.94%), Kami (77.98%) and Halakhor (77.89%). Again in 2001 also following sub-caste groups are possess highest literacy rate, they are—Konowr (82.95%), Sunri (82.28%), Dhoba, Dhubi (73.93%), Kandra (72.15%), Pod, Poundra (72.10%), Namasudra (71.93%), Damai (69.83%), Kadar (69.74%), Kami (68.78%) and Halakhor (68.69%). In the census 1991 following sub groups' people having the highest literacy rate, they are—Sunri (65.96%), Dhobi (62.07%), Kandra (60.09%), Konowr (58.37%), Namasudra (56.18%), Pan Sawasi (54.82%), Dabgar (52.84%), Damai (52.44%), Baiti (51.93%), Halalkhor (51.47%). In the other hand the lowest literacy groups are Musahar (15.25%), Ghasi (30.45%), Bantar (33.11%), Barui (37.46%), Debgar (34.51%), Bind (35.01%), Mal (39.63%), Beldar (39.79%), Paliya (41.84%) and Koch (42.96%). In 1991 census the lowest literacy groups are—Mushahar (15.75%), Bind (20.76), Barui (21.47%), Khaira (24.20%), Mal (26.56%), Ghasi (26.45%), Turi (27.62%), Koch (28.71%), Lohar (29.75%) and Dom (29.09%). So, from the report it is reveals that literacy among the same community groups are very common among the scheduled caste in West Bengal. Some of groups were better in the census 1991, but they could not maintain their growth rate; in the same way some of them were not better but later on they could draw attention of the nation through their literacy performance in the state. In the following Table 1.5 literacy variation among different community groups of scheduled caste in various years are shown from 1961-2011.

The scheduled caste literacy rate in West Bengal is 68.24 per cent, this limit crossed by the following community groups. They are—Sunri, Sarki, Bahelia, Baiti, Damai, Dhoba, Doai, Doshad, Halakhor, jalia Kaibarta, Jhalo Malo, Kadar, Kanjar, Kandra, Khatik, Konwar, Kotal, lalbegi, Namasudra, Nat, Pan, Pasi, Rajbanshi, Patni, Pod and Tiyr; and rest of the community groups lies below of the measuring line in the state.

Table 1.5: Distribution of Literacy Rate among Different Communities of Scheduled Caste in West Bengal from 1961-2011

Sl No.	*State/Districts*	*1961*	*1971*	*1981*	*1991*	*2001*	*2011**
1.	All Scheduled Castes	13.58	17.80	24.42	42.21	59.04	68.26
2.	Bagdi, Duley	8.74	10.79	13.96	30.02	47.72	56.92
3.	Bahelia	11.56	14.39	22.53	39.21	59.61	68.81
4.	Baiti	12.72	17.99	32.92	51.93	68.84	78.04
5..	Bantar	15.40	18.05	17.73	35.19	33.11	42.31
6.	Bauri	5.47	10.11	9.42	21.47	37.46	46.66
7.	Beldar	9.64	20.21	18.70	31.91	39.79	48.99
8.	Bhogta	3.14	33.33	18.03	35.91	47.89	57.09
9.	Bhuimali	11.32	17.41	21.22	39.63	57.13	66.33
10	Bhuiya	7.07	9.95	14.22	33.84	42.09	51.29
11.	Bind	6.57	10.86	12.70	20.76	35.01	44.21
12.	Chamar, Charmakar, Mochi, Muchi, Rabidas, Ruidas, Rishi	8.34	12.00	14.42	28.08	46.99	56.19
13.	Chaupal	3.25	16.34	20.76	28.52	43.15	52.35
14.	Dabgar	29.17	20.43	22.39	52.84	34.51	43.71
15.	Damai (Nepali)	21.07	37.25	37.46	52.44	69.83	79.03
16.	Dhoba, Dhobi	18.92	24.28	38.79	62.07	73.87	83.07
17.	Doai	6.23	17.32	22.55	47.11	60.09	69.29
18.	Dom, Dhangad	7.06	9.88	12.58	29.09	46.02	55.22
19.	Dosadh, Dusadh, Dhari, Dharhi	12.92	16.67	23.67	44.23	59.56	68.76
20.	Ghasi	5.82	10.19	9.01	26.55	30.45	39.65
21.	Gonrhi	5.64	18.61	25.21	37.87	56.04	65.24
22.	Halalkhor	24.54	10.43	29.90	51.47	68.69	77.89
23.	Hari, Mehtar, Mehtor, Bhangi	7.69	10.77	15.28	42.10	49.45	58.65
24.	Jalia Kaibartta	17.95	20.47	30.16	49.31	64.85	74.05
25.	Jhalo Malo, Malo	14.50	19.18	25.51	42.52	60.33	69.53
26.	Kadar	12.16	22.81	25.50	30.75	69.74	78.94
27.	Kami (Nepali)	18.05	27.91	34.70	49.45	68.78	77.98
28.	Kandra	15.11	24.02	31.49	60.09	72.15	81.35
29.	Kanjar	16.16	8.18	16.03	32.45	65.35	74.55
30.	Kaora	9.65	17.30	17.81	32.32	52.99	62.19
31.	Karenga, Koranga	9.48	12.33	18.39	35.68	54.81	64.01
32.	Kaur	12.33	14.47	16.46	38.72	52.14	61.34
33.	Keot, Keyot	13.81	16.57	23.21	41.75	53.79	62.99
34.	Khaira	5.33	9.17	10.98	24.20	42.28	51.48
35.	Khatik	25.33	17.96	30.01	42.11	68.94	78.14
36.	Koch	8.57	16.13	15.19	28.71	42.96	52.16
37.	Konai	7.40	9.06	15.91	30.57	49.65	58.85
38.	Konwar	15.66	24.50	45.69	58.37	82.95	92.15
39.	Kotal	12.48	14.44	21.75	45.35	59.69	68.89
40.	Kurariar	5.40	21.95	25.14	42.20	56.72	65.92
41.	Lalbegi	18.11	21.53	25.87	51.82	67.15	76.35
42.	Lohar	8.30	12.37	15.09	29.73	46.50	55.70
43.	Mahar	11.79	13.35	19.85	40.26	52.60	61.80
44.	Mal	5.91	9.58	12.16	26.56	39.63	48.83

(Contd.)

Sl No.	State/Districts	1961	1971	1981	1991	2001	*2011
45.	Mallah	14.06	15.41	23.80	37.65	53.86	63.06
46.	Musahar	3.16	8.28	5.30	15.75	15.25	24.45
47.	Namasudra	21.03	26.86	35.87	56.18	71.93	81.13
48.	Nat	4.45	39.19	31.25	49.67	59.25	68.45
49.	Nuniya	11.02	15.85	20.75	39.39	54.19	63.39
50.	Paliya	11.63	20.88	18.46	30.96	41.84	51.04
51.	Pan, Sawasi	16.91	16.37	27.25	54.91	61.00	70.20
52.	Pasi	15.61	7.89	26.79	46.32	64.11	73.31
53.	Patni	16.19	18.93	25.44	49.40	64.49	73.69
54.	Pod, Poundra	21.68	27.31	36.49	56.05	72.10	81.30
55.	Rajbanshi	14.75	17.56	24.65	40.71	60.14	69.34
56.	Rajwar	9.17	11.36	16.63	38.68	46.41	55.61
57.	Sarki (Nepali)	14.35	26.02	27.32	49.30	62.48	71.68
58.	Sunri (Excluding Saha	28.58	22.41	54.95	65.96	82.28	91.48
59.	Tiyar	8.06	20.40	25.33	45.16	62.11	71.31
60.	Turi	7.48	12.95	14.25	27.62	40.59	49.79
61.	Unclassified	15.01	20.20	-	37.39	62.19	71.39

*Projected data.
Source: Census reports of India, RGI 1961-2001.

Educational Scenario of Namasudra in West Bengal

The Namasudras are very strong scheduled caste group in West Bengal. They shared second position in the scheduled caste population of West Bengal; they share 17.40 per cent to the total scheduled caste of the state according to the census 2001 of West Bengal. Namasudras are the indigenous group people of the state. In all the districts of Bengal this group of are found in different number. In the following Table 1.6 the numbers of Namasudra people are shown during the years 1991 and 2001 census of West Bengal.

The number of population of this group is growing day by day. The number growing population may shown by the following table, which is prepared from all census report of the state.

From the table it is found that up to the census 1941 the growth rate of total population of Namasudra in West Bengal had in one trend but after 1951 their growth rate suddenly change, which may be the cause of separation of the country after independence. Because after independence of the country large number of Hindu population came to India from East Pakistan (presently Bangladesh); and due to that the population of India got affected.

The Namasudra people in West Bengal are to some extent develop in the field of education in comparison to the other community group among scheduled caste of the state. Their present literacy rate is

Table 1.6: Namasudra Population from 1872-2001 in West Bengal

Year	*Namasudra Population*
1872	201,745
1881	168,872
1891	195,353
1901	174,888
1911	160,304
1921	165,027
1931	161,804
1941	134,748
1951	324,723
1961	817,280
1971	980,524
1981	16,92,233
1991	25,81,549
2001	32,12,393

Source: (i) Census 1951 West Bengal, The Tribes and Castes of West Bengal, by A. Mitra, Govt. Press, Alipore, West Bengal, 1953.
(ii) Census of West Bengal, 1961, 1971, 1981, 1991 and 2001.

71.93 per cent, which is fifth position out of the 59 sub-community of the scheduled castes group in the state. In the census 1961 of West Bengal their literacy rate was 21.03 per cent, 26.86 per cent in 1971, 35.87 per cent in 1981, 56.18 per cent in 1991, 71.93 per cent in 2001 and 81.13 per cent in 2011. The present literacy rate of the group is higher than the state level scheduled castes literacy rate. It is also reveal from the table above that the literacy rate of the Namasudra people is higher than the all census report in West Bengal, 1961, 1971, 1981, 1991, 2001 and 2011. This progress in the field of education reveals that the Namasudra people in West Bengal are developing with pace of the development of the society as well as country.

As it is mentioned above that Namasudra people are found all the districts of West Bengal; but their academic developments are not equal in all the districts.

CONSTITUTIONAL PROVISIONS OF SCHEDULED CASTE IN INDIA

After getting independence Govt. of India adopted the constitution for execute the country smoothly. Independence ushered in a new era of national development based on the acceptance of a socialistic pattern of society which would secure equitable distribution of wealth and equality of opportunity for all, without any distinction of caste, race, religion, sex or place of birth in education, employment and cultural development.

The Directive Principles of State Policy include universal education to all children up to the age of 14 years, promotion, with special care, of the educational and economic interests of the weaker sections of the people, and in particular, of the Scheduled Castes and Scheduled Tribes, and protection from social injustice and all forms of exploitation. The constitution has also made safeguards to protect the interests of the Scheduled Castes and Scheduled Tribes against any injustice in the matter of establishment of admission to educational institutions and grants from State funds. Constitutional provisions regarding Scheduled Castes education may be mentioned in the following ways –

Articles 15(4), 29, 30, 45-46 and 350-A are the relevant provisions in the constitution pertaining to educational development of the people. While Article 29 relates to protection of interests of minorities, Articles 30 deals with rights of minorities to establish and administer educational institution which also figure under a separate heading 'Cultural and Educational Rights' in the Fundamental Rights chapter of the constitution.

In the chapter on Directive Principles of State Policy, there is a direction in Article 45 of the Constitution enjoins that:

> The State shall Endeavour to provide, within a period of ten years from the commencement of this Constitution, for free and compulsory education for all children until they complete the age of fourteen years.

Article 45 declares the objective of the State, and like other Directives, does not confer any justifiable right. Though the Courts are not competent to compel the Government to carry out the Directive or to make any law for that purpose, for example, to provide for free and compulsory education within the time limited by Article 45, this Article nevertheless castes a duty on the State to follow both in the matter of administration as well as in the matter of laws.

Article 15(4) finds place in the Fundamental Rights chapter of the Constitution while Article 45 and 46 have been included in the chapter on Directive Principles of the State Policy.

Article 15(4) provides that, "Nothing in this article or in clause (2) of Article 29 shall prevent the State from making any special provision for the advancement of any socially and educationally backward classes of citizens or for the Scheduled Castes and the Scheduled Tribes.

The object of Clause (4) of Article 15, added in 1951 by the constitution (first Amendment) Act, 1951, is to bring Articles 15 and 29 in line with articles 16(4), 46 and 340, and to make it constitutional for the state to reserve seats for backward classes of citizens, scheduled castes and scheduled tribes in the Public educational institutions, as well as to make other special provisions as may be necessary for their advancement.

Article 15(4) speaks of 'classes of citizens' for whom the state can make special provisions to promote, scholars to the detriment if they are socially and educationally backward. The Scheduled Castes and Scheduled Tribes, however, constitute a protected class, apart from any condition of backwardness, as specified, in Article 15(4). Hence, the state is entitled to do everything for the upliftment of members of these castes and tribes, to make restorations for their admission to educational institution and to impose such conditions or would make the reservation effective. Additionally, Article 16(4) speaks of reservation of appointment/ posts of SC's and STs.

Articles 15(4) and 16(4) are characterized by the purpose of special provisions. Not merely confirming special privileges on the backward classes, but as serving the interests of the Whole society by promoting the advancement of the weaker elements.

In the chapter on 'Directive Principles of state policy', there is a direction in *Article 46* which postulates;

> "The state shall promote with special care the educational and economic interests of the weaker sections of the people, and in particular, of the scheduled castes and the scheduled tribes and shall protect them from social injustice and all forms of exploitation."

Article 17 The abolition of 'untouchability' and the forbidding of its practice in any form.

Article 25 The throwing open of Hindu religious institutions of a public character to all classes and sections of Hindus.

Article 19 The right to practice any profession or carry on any occupation, trade or business.

Article 29 The forbidding of any denial of admission to educational institutions maintained by the states or receiving aid out of the state funds.

Article 16 and 335 The obligation of the State to consider their claims in the making of appointments to public services and reservation for them in case of inadequate representation.

Article 330, 332 and 334 provide special representation in parliament and State Legislatures for a period of twenty years.

Article 164, 338 and fifth schedule of the constitution assure for setting up of advisory councils and separate departments in the state and the appointment of a Special Official at the Centre to promote their welfare and safeguard their interests.

Article 2 and Fifth and sixth schedule provide special provision for the administration and control of schedule and tribal areas.

RECOMMENDATIONS OF COMMISSION AND COMMITTEES ON DEVELOPMENT OF THE SCHEDULED CASTE

Scheduled Caste population constitutes 16 per cent of the total population of the country at present, but this group people are considered as backward, because they are lag behind regarding their socio-economic and educational aspects in the society. After independence of India Government of India adopted different steps, policies to develop this backward community in the country. Besides these, in different times different committees and commission are also constituted to recommendation regarding the development of Scheduled Castes. Some of such commissions and committees are mention bellow –

(1) The Committee appointed to inquire into the Educational, Economic and Social Conditions of the Depressed Classes and the aboriginal Tribes in the Bombay Presidency, 1930. This is one of the oldest reports on this important subject and a historical landmark. The Bharat Ratna Dr. Babàsaheb Ambedkar was the distinguished member of this Committee.

(2) Report of the Commissioner for Scheduled Castes and Scheduled Tribes 1951-52, Report. New Delhi, Office of the National Commissioner for Scheduled Castes/Scheduled Tribes. The report of the Commissioner for Scheduled Castes and Scheduled Tribes, published annually, is perhaps the most extensive document in terms of its coverage of the various aspects of the existential condition of the Scheduled Castes and Scheduled Tribes.

(3) The Backward Classes Commission, 1955 appointed by the president, in pursuance of Article 340, appointed the Backward Classes Commission.

(4) Under the chairmanship of M.P. Bhargava constitute *The Special Group on co-operation for Backward Classes in 1961.* By setting up this committee Ministry of Home Affairs wanted to study the progress of Backward Classes, particularly the Scheduled Castes and Scheduled Tribes, in the field of cooperation in the first and Second Five Year Plans and to suggest measures for accelerating the progress in this field during the Third Five Year Plan.

(5) The Education Commission 1964 was appointed by the Government of India by Resolution, dated 14th July, 1964 to advise Government on the national pattern of education and on the general principles and policies for the development of education at all stages and in all aspects. The Committee recommended that the existing programme for the education of the Scheduled Castes should continue be the expanded. Greater efforts are needed to provide educational facilities for the nomadic and semi-nomadic groups. Hostel facilities should be provided for the children of the denotified communities. The education of the tribal people deserves great emphasis and attention. Commission broadly agree with the recommendations made in this respect by the Commission on Scheduled Castes and Scheduled Tribes under the chairmanship of Shri U.N. Dhebar and in the seminars on the Education and Employment of the Tribal people organized by the Planning Commission and the NCERT.

(6) In 1965 under chairmanship of Elyayaperumal, L. on Untouchability, Economic and Educational Development of the Scheduled Castes and connected Documents was constituted under the Department of Social Welfare. Terms of reference of the committee were—

(i) to study the various aspects of untouchability, in particular the working of the untouchability Act. 1955, and the restrictions, if any imposed on the entry of Harijans into public places of working and to suggest remedial measures;

(ii) to study the problem of the economic uplift of the Scheduled Castes, evaluate the impact of the present schemes, and make recommendations as to the further measures that may be necessary; and

(iii) to study the problems of education of Scheduled Castes, assess the progress achieved so far and suggest further measures that may be necessary.

Committee recommended in part III of the report to increase the enrolment of Scheduled Caste children in schools, the services of Gram Sevaks and Panchayat Presidents and officers may be utilized. It is futile to make elementary education compulsory if simultaneous efforts are not made to induce the parents to send their children to school. First of all, a proper field should be prepared by providing such incentives as mid-day meals, free supply of books, stationary, etc. and then only education should be made compulsory by legislation.

Lack of schooling facilities near to the villages is an all-India problem found in all the states except few. In a country like India, where majority of the population lives in villages, especially Scheduled Castes; it is high time for the State Governments to change their policy of preferential treatment to towns and cities in the establishment of educational institutions. As all the states facing same problem, this matter deserves immediate attention of Government authorities.

Scheduled Caste individuals coming up for establishing educational institutions should be given all facilities such as free land, building grant of at least 50 per cent of the expenditure etc. All such institutions should be attached with hostels and such facilities as mentioned above should be given for establishing hostels also.

The Committee feels that the present rate of scholarship is quite inadequate in the present increased cost of living condition.

Scheduled caste students should be exempted from payment of all special fees such as game fee, laboratory fee, examination fee, library fee, etc.

Necessary arrangement should be made by the Government to supply set of costly text-books to students on loan basis as is being done by the Tamil Nadu Government through Welfare Department.

A uniform procedure should be adopted by all the State Governments for implementation of the scheme and disbursement of scholarship amounts. The Department of Social Welfare to which post-matric scholarship scheme has been transferred recently should evolve a uniform procedure for disbursement of grants, acceptable to all the State Governments.

A separate form of application should be prescribed for Scheduled Castes and other Backward Classes.

State Governments should introduce Overseas Scholarship Scheme in their state to benefit Scheduled Castes students who possess good academic qualifications.

In the case of Scheduled Castes student admitted in private general hostels all their expenses should be met by the Government and stipends scholarship be increased for this purpose.

Untouchability and segregation in any form should not be allowed to continue in any of the hostels fun by Government of Voluntary Organization.

The Central Government should directly construct, at least some hostels in each State to accommodate needy Scheduled Caste students.

Preference should be given by the State Governments for construction of Scheduled Caste Girl's Hostels.

All stipends/scholarships including post-matric scholarships should be fixed at higher rates say at least at Rs. 10 p.m. more for girls, than for boys. This is essential in view of the higher expenditure of girl students compared to boys.

Girls traveling to distant places by buses/trains etc. should be paid their actual conveyance charges.

Overseas scholarships, passes grants, scholarships for study in Public Schools etc. should be awarded to all qualified Scheduled Caste woman apply for the same.

In some districts in states, as an experimental measure a least one primary/middle/high school with attached hostels should be opened for education of Scheduled Caste girls.

Education of girls should be work oriented. In middle and high school classes, special training may be imparted in weaving, tailoring, typing, shorthand, etc.

(7) In 1986 National Policy on Education was constituted by the Government of India to strengthen the educational situation of the country. This policy recommended to the all sectors of education including Scheduled Castes and Scheduled Tribes and Backward Classes people of the country. In the National policy on Education, the following special provisions for Scheduled Caste and Scheduled Tribes have been incorporated in the existing schemes of the Departments of Elementary Education and Literacy and Secondary and Higher Education—

I. Relaxed norms for opening of primary schools.
II. A primary school within one km walking distance from habitations of 200 populations instead of habitations of 300 populations.
III. Abolition of tuition fee in all States in Government schools at least up to upper primary level. Most of the states have abolished tuition fee for SC/ST students up to senior secondary level.
IV. Provision of incentives like free text books, uniforms, stationary, school bags, etc., to these students.
V. The major programmes of the Department of Education, viz., *Sarva Shiksha Abhiyan* (SSA), District Primary Education Programme (DPEP), *Lok Jumbish (LJ), Shiksha Karmi (SK),* and National Programme for Nutritional Support to Primary Education accord priority to areas of concentration of SCs and STs.

VI. Reservation of seats for SCs and STs in Central Government institutions of higher education including IITs, IIMs, Regional Engineering Colleges, Central Universities, Kendriya Vidyalayas, Navodaya Vidyalayas, etc. There is also relaxation in the minimum qualifying cut-off stages for admission to Universities, Colleges and Technical institutions, apart from reservation. The UGC has established SC/ST Cells in 104 Universities including Central Universities, to ensure proper implementation of the reservation policy.

VII. To improve academic skills and linguistic proficiency of students in various subjects and to raise their level of comprehension, remedial and special coaching is provided to SC/ST students.

VIII. SC/ST candidates are provided relaxation up to 10 per cent in the cut off marks for the Junior Research Fellowship (JRF) test and all the SC and ST candidates qualify for JRF are awarded scholarships.

IX. Fifty Junior Fellowships are awarded every year in Sciences and Humanities including Social Sciences to SC/ST candidates who appear in the National Eligibility Test (NET) and qualify for Lectureship.

X. The University Grant Commission provides a relaxation of 5 per cent at the Master's Level for appointment as Lecturer for SC/ST candidates.

So from the above discussion it is seen that Government of India has taken lots of initiative to strengthen the academic position of the Scheduled Caste population in the country.

SPECIAL PROVISIONS OF SCHEDULED CASTES

After independence, the Government of India has taken number of steps to strengthen the educational base of the persons belonging to the Scheduled Castes and Scheduled Tribes. Pursuant to the National Policy on Education-1986 and the Programme of Action (POA) 1992, the following special provisions for SCs and STs have been incorporated in the existing schemes of the Departments of Elementary Education and Literacy and Secondary and Higher Education:

(a) relaxed norms for opening of primary/middle schools; a primary school within one km walking distance from habitations of population upto 200 instead of habitations of upto 300 population.

(b) Abolition of tuition fee in all States in Government Schools at least upto the upper primary level.

In fact, most of the states have abolished tuition fees for SC/ST students up to the senior secondary level. (c) Incentives like free textbooks, uniforms, stationery, schools bags, etc., for these students. (d) The Constitutional (86th Amendment) Bill, notified on 13 December 2002, provides for free and compulsory elementary education as a Fundamental Right, for all children in the age group of 6-14 years. (e) Sarva Shiksha Abhiyan (SSA): SSA is a historic stride towards achieving the long cherished goal of Universalisation of Elementary Education (UEE) through a time bound integrated approach, in partnership with States. SSA, which promises to change the face of elementary education sector of the country, aims to provide useful and quality elementary education to all children in the 6-14 age group by 2010. The main features of the programme are: (i) Focus on girls, especially belonging to SC/ST communities and minority groups. (ii) Back to school campus for out of school girls. (iii) Free textbooks for girls. (iv) Special coaching remedial classes for girls and a congenial learning environment. (v) Teachers' sensitisation programmes to promote equitable learning opportunities. (vi) Special focus for innovative projects related to girls education. (vii) Recruitment of 50 per cent female teachers.

District Primary Education Programme (DPEP)

The thrust of the scheme is on disadvantaged groups like girls, SCs/STs, working children, urban deprived children, disabled children, etc. There are specific strategies for girls and SCs/STs; however, physical targets are fixed, in an integrated manner including coverage of these groups as well. According to a study by NIEPA, schools in DPEP districts had more than 60 per cent students belonging to SC/ST communities.

Mahila Samakhya (MS)

MS addresses traditional gender imbalances in educational access and achievement. This involves enabling women (especially from socially and economically disadvantaged and marginalised groups) to address and deal with problems of isolation and lack of self-confidence, oppressive social customs and struggle for survival, all of which inhibit their empowerment.

National Programme for Education of Girls at Elementary Level (NPEGEL)

The NPEGEL under the existing scheme of Sarva Shiksha Abhiyan (SSA) provides additional components for education of girls under privileged/ disadvantaged at the elementary level. The Scheme is being implemented in Educationally Backward Blocks (EBBs) where the level of rural female literacy is less than the national average and the gender gap is above the national average, as well as in blocks of districts that have at least 5 per cent SC/ST population and where SC/ST female literacy is below 10 per cent based on 1991.

Shiksha Karmi Project (SKP)

SKP aims at universalisation and qualitative improvement of primary education in remote, arid and socio-economically backward villages in Rajasthan with primary attention to girls. It is noteworthy that in Shiksha Karmi Schools, most of the students are from SCs, STs and OBCs. Kasturba Gandhi Balika Vidyalayas: Under the scheme of Kasturba Gandhi Balika Vidyalaya, 750 residential schools are being set up in difficult areas with boarding facilities at elementary level for girls belonging predominantly to the SC, ST, OBC and minorities. The scheme would be applicable only in those identified Educationally Backward Blocks (EBBs) where, as per census data 2001, the rural female literacy is below the national average and gender gap in literacy is more than the national average. Among these blocks, schools may be set up in areas with concentration of tribal population, with low female literacy and/or a large number of girls out of school.

Jan Shikshan Sansthan (JSS)

The Scheme of JSS or Institute of People's Education is a polyvalent or multifaceted adult education programme aimed at improving the vocational skill and quality of life of the beneficiaries. The objective of the scheme is education, vocational and occupational development of the socio-economically backward and educationally disadvantaged groups of urban/rural population particularly neo-literates, semi-illiterates, SCs, STs, women and girls, slum dwellers, migrant workers, etc. Literacy campaigns have had an enormous impact on other social sectors. The campaigns have served the cause of promoting equity and social justice in society and fostering of a scientific temper and a sense of belonging to India's great composite culture and consciousness of unity in diversity.

Mid-Day Meal scheme: The Mid-Day Meal scheme is a successful incentive programme. It covers all students of primary classes in all government, local body and government aided schools in the country with the aim to improve enrolment, attendance and retention while simultaneously impacting on the nutritional status of the children. The Central Institute of Indian Languages (CIIL), Mysore has a scheme of development of Indian Languages through research, developing manpower and production of materials in modern Indian Languages including tribal languages. The Institute has worked in more than 90 tribal and border languages.

Kendriya Vidyalayas (KVS)

15 per cent and 7.5 per cent seats are reserved for SCs and STs respectively in fresh admissions. No tuition fee is charged from scheduled Caste and Scheduled Tribe students up to class XII.

Navodaya Vidyalayas (NVS)

Reservation of seats in favour of children belonging to SCs and STs is provided in proportion to their population in the concerned district provided that no such reservation will be less than the national average of 22.5 per cent (15% for SCs and 7.50% for STs) and a maximum of 50 per cent for both the categories (SCs and STs) taken together. These reservations are interchangeable and over and above the students selected under open merit.

SCHOLARSHIP SCHEME FOR SC/ST CANDIDATES

Dr. Ambedkar National Scholarship Scheme for meritorious students, is implemented by Dr. Ambedkar Foundation set up under the aegis of the Ministry of Social Justice and Empowerment in 1992 with a view to recognize, promote and assist meritorious students belonging to Scheduled Caste and Scheduled Tribe for enabling them to pursue higher studies. This is one time cash award and will be given to three students scoring highest marks in the regular class X level examination conducted by the Education Board/Council. This will be separate for SC and ST.

In case none of the first three eligible students are girls, the girl students scoring the highest mark will get a special award. As and when asked by the Ministry of Social Welfare and Justice, NIOS is supposed to send the names of eligible candidates for this scheme. Under the Scheme of strengthening of Boarding and Hostel Facilities for Girl Students of Secondary and Higher Secondary Schools cent percent financial assistance is given to Voluntary Organisations to improve enrolment of adolescent girls belonging to rural areas and weaker sections.

Preference is given to educationally backward districts particularly those predominately inhabited by SCs/STs and educationally backward minorities. Out of 43,000 scholarships at the secondary stage for talented children from rural areas 13,000 scholarships are awarded to SC/ST students subject to fulfilment of criteria laid down.

RATIONALE OF THE STUDY

Since independence, the Government of India has been provided some constitutional safeguard to the people who are socially, economically and culturally backward. The objective of such a policy is to benefit the weaker sections of the society. This has been administered by the Central and State Governments. It tries to remove social and religious inabilities of the lower caste. It provides facilities in education, employment, parliament, state legislators and locals' bodies and finally, the policy safeguards the deprived class from all sorts of social injustice and exploitation. In the way spirit a number of research studies has been carried out in this section of people to find out their status, problems in various levels by the numbers of administrators, different organizations, NGOs, research scholar, social thinkers, academicians and others. Their main objective was to find out some solution to abolish the gap between scheduled caste and non-scheduled caste and welfare of the scheduled caste people in Indian society.

For the development of the scheduled caste in India, the Government has given a special importance to provide educational opportunities. The central focus in the SC's educational development is of their equalization with the non-SC population at all stages and levels of education in all areas and in all the four dimensions—rural male, rural female, urban male and urban female. There are approximately 14 crores of Scheduled Caste populations in India. Scheduled caste population constitutes 16.41 per cent population in the country. This now take us to the question of their educational development. How fare these population are provided with educational facilities and how far developmental indicators have been ascertained is to be examined. Unfortunately studies in the Education of Scheduled Caste did not attract attention of Scholars as much as that of Scheduled Tribes. Parliamentary debate on the Golden Jubilee of Independence reveals that we have failed to bring about large-scale reforms in the condition of SC's and ST's even after 50 years of independence. The benefits of the plans and programmes made for the augmentation of the SC's and ST's had not reached them. We had failed to abolish untouchability and it was still practiced. Further, the advantage of reservation did not reach the target groups. There are wide variations in the percentage of enrolment ratio (between SC's and non-SC's) among the various States and Union Territories of the country. There are also wide variations in literacy percentage among different districts as well as among different scheduled caste groups within the states. Again some of the states specially West Bengal claims that untouchability and inequality has been reduced and government policies are implemented but the recent report of Nobel Laureate Prof. Amartya Sen reveals that the situation is in no way better than the earlier time. Education facilities of the scheduled caste people are distressed.

Of course, it is gratifying to note that although ICSSR has initiated such survey's, yet, it needs to emphasis that the national survey should be supplement by intensive studies of the individual scheduled caste groups to gain a clear and comprehensive understanding of the problems and prospects of the SC education in different regions. The Central focus in the Scheduled Castes' educational development in the NPE' 86 and in revised NPE 92, is their equalization with non-SC population at all stages and levels of education.

But hardly any study has been carried out to find out the gap between the constitutional and policy commitment and of its implementation. Only the commission of SC/ST in its report (1986-87) has reviewed the constitutional schemes for the advancement of SC/ST's and their implementation during the plan periods. The report also brings out some of the salient points related to the educational development of SC/ST with special reference being made to accessibility of schools drop out ratio at various level of schooling and enrolment ratios. The review of the researches revealed that a single study has not been carried out with regard to the policy implementation of the educational development of scheduled caste, specially. Further it is a matter of regret that not even a single study has been taken up about the development of education of the Scheduled caste in North East India and also in a comparative perspective with other states. Because the glomming picture of the development of scheduled caste education hinders of educational progress as a whole. If 16 per cent of the populations are unable to participate in the development process how can there be advancement in the country. It appears that hardly any study has been carried out on the SC population with special reference to any specific community. It pursued the researcher to raise the following questions.

1. What is the extent of participation in education of scheduled caste communities in West Bengal?
2. What is the extent of participation in education of Namasudra community in West Bengal?
3. What are the problems of Namasudra community in West Bengal with regard to education?
4. How do parents, students and community members of Namasudra community in West Bengal perceive education?
5. How can equitable participation in education of different castes within the scheduled communities be ensured?

REFERENCES

Aggarwal, Y. and *et al.* (1994), *Educating Scheduled Castes, NIEPA*, New Delhi, pp. 1-2.

Bhuimali, A. and Laha, S.S. (2007), Genesis of Scheduled Castes and Constitutional Safeguards for them, *Development of Scheduled Caste* (Ed), Anil Bhuimali, Serial Publications, New Delhi, p. 174.

Chakraborty, B. (2007), Literacy rate among the Scheduled Castes with reference to West Bengal, *Development of scheduled caste (Ed.)*, by Anil Bhuimali, Serials Publications, New Delhi, p. 179.

Chakraborty, B. (2007), Literacy rate among the Scheduled Castes with reference to West Bengal, *Development of Scheduled Caste (Ed.)*, by Anil Bhuimali, Serials Publications, New Delhi, p. 177.

Chatterjee, S.K. (2000), *Educational Development of Scheduled Castes: Looking Ahead*, Gyan Publishing House, New Delhi, p. 1.

Chatterjee, S.K. (2000), *Educational Development of Scheduled Castes Looking Ahead*, Gyan Publishing House, New Delhi, p. 5.

Dubey, S.M. (1975), *Study of Schedueld caste and Scheduled Tribe students in Assam*, (Project report) Dibrugarh University, Dibrugarh.

Ibid., p. 376.

Ibid., p. 377.

Ibid., p. 386.

Ibid., p. 389.

Ibid., p. 390.

Ibid., p. 391.

Ibid., p. 7.

Ibid., p. 9.
Ibid., pp. 387-388.
Laha, S.S. and Anil Bhuimali (2007), Genesis of Scheduled Castes and Constitutional Safeguards for them in *Development of scheduled caste (Ed.)*, by Anil Bhuimali, Serials Publications, New Delhi, p. 161.
Malhotra, N. and Rizvi, N. (1997), *Source Material on Education of Scheduled Castes and Scheduled Tribes*, Anamika Publishers and Distributors (P) Ltd., Delhi, p. 373.
Saxena, N.R.S. and Chaturbedi, S. (2006), *Teacher in Emerging Indian Society*, R. Lall Book Depot, Meerut, pp. 538-539.
The Scheduled Caste in India, S.K. Chatterjee, Gyan Publishing House, New Delhi, p. 249.
Various Censuses of India, (West Bengal), Years 1961-2001.

II

Scheduled Castes in West Bengal

The Scheduled Castes are the people who belong to the last Varna namely the Shudra or Avarna or Antyaja. The expression "Scheduled Castes" was first used by the Simon Commission and embodied in the Government of India Act of 1935. Before 1935 they were known as untouchables or exterior castes or depressed castes. Indian society is based on the institution of castes. Caste system in India is not a new phenomenon. Caste system in India was found in the traditional Hindu society. The institution of caste has survived in India in a far better form than any other country of the world. It is found in Egypt, in Polynesia, in Melanesia, in Fiji, in Somalia, in Rwanda, and in many other countries. In ancient Greece and Rome too caste system was noticed in a comparable form. Traces of caste can also be found in Western Asia, China, Japan, America, Rome and Tribal India.

"Caste" forms an important social Unit of the Hindu Social System. Its influence has also been observed amongst other religious groups. A good deal of controversy still exists relating to the origin of Caste system in India. However, it is believed that the very core of casteism was prevalent among the Australoid population. Subsequent racial mixture with the migrating Aryan speaking population gave a concrete shape to the caste system. The caste system has undergone changes through decades and taken different shapes in different parts of India as per local tradition, history and environment. The racial mixture between different groups (Australoid, Proto-Australoid, Aryan speaking, etc) gave raise to institution of 'Untouchability' in the historic past. During the British period, the terms like "Depressed Caste", "Exterior Caste", "Backward Caste", "Scheduled Caste", etc. were used to denote some castes. During pre-Independence period, no significant step was taken for the socio-economic development of the scheduled castes, excepting few educational grants, etc. But after Independence realizing the gravity of the problems several provisions have been made in the Constitution of the Republic of India for giving safeguard to the scheduled castes people. As per Article 46 of the constitution, State Government have also launched various programmes concerning the development of the scheduled castes and scheduled tribes.

After independence of India our Constitution has offered some social, economic and political safeguards to the section of people who belong to Scheduled Caste category. According to the Census data, the percentage of scheduled caste population was 14.82 per cent in 1971, 15.75 per cent in 1981, 16.48 per cent in 1991 and 16.20 (total, 166635700) percent in 2001. Out of this total scheduled caste population, more than 90 per cent live in rural areas and only less than 10 per cent people are live in urban areas. In the following Table 2.1 distribution of scheduled caste population in different States in India is given below.

From the table it is found that out of 35 states (including Union Territories) maximum Scheduled Castes population are found in the states Uttar Pradesh (35148377), West Bengal (18452555), Bihar (13048608), Andhra Pradesh (12339496), Tamil Nadu (11857504), Maharashtra (9881656), Rajasthan (9644462) and Madhya Pradesh (9155177) and lowest population found in the states Mizoram (272), Dadra and Nagar Haveli (4104), Daman and Diu (4838), Arunachal Pradesh (6188), Meghalaya (11139), Goa (23791) and Sikkim (27165). Of these states in three states there is no Scheduled Caste population which are—Andaman and Nicobar Islands, Lakshadweep, Nagaland.

In India out of 35 States, 32 States comprise scheduled caste population in a certain proportion with the general population. Again it is very important to mention that numbers of sub-community of scheduled castes group are different in state to state. There are 578 different castes have been enlisted in the category of scheduled castes in different state of the country. The number of scheduled caste communities are varies from state to state, viz.—Andhra Pradesh (59), Arunachal Pradesh (16), Assam (16), Bihar (23), Goa (5), Gujarat (30), Haryana (37), Himachal Pradesh (56), Jammu and Kashmir (13), Karnataka (101), Kerala (68), Madhya Pradesh (47), Maharashtra (59), Manipur (7), Meghalaya (16), Mizoram (16), Orissa (93), Punjab (37), Rajasthan (59), Sikkim (4), Tamil Nadu (76), Tripura (32), Uttar Pradesh (66), West Bengal (59), Chandigarh (36), Dadra and Nagar Haveli (4), Daman and Diu (5), Delhi (36) and Pondicherry (15).

Table 2.1: Distribution of Scheduled Caste Population in States of India According to Census 2001

Sl No.	*State/Districts*	*Male*	*Female*	*Total*	*% of SC*
1.	Andhra Pradesh	6228011	6111485	12339496	16.19
2.	Arunachal Pradesh	3590	2598	6188	0.56
3.	Assam	943674	882275	1825949	6.85
4.	Bihar	6784676	6263932	13048608	15.72
5.	Chhattisgarh	1213194	1205528	2418722	11.61
6.	Goa	12047	11744	23791	1.77
7.	Gujarat	1866283	1726432	3592715	7.09
8.	Haryana	2188585	1902525	4091110	19.35
9.	Himachal Pradesh	763333	738837	1502170	24.72
10.	Jammu and Kashmir	403256	366899	770155	7.59
11.	Jharkhand	1640583	1548737	3189320	11.84
12.	Karnataka	4339745	4224185	8563930	16.20
13.	Kerala	1525114	1598827	3123941	9.81
14.	Madhya Pradesh	4804881	4350296	9155177	15.71
15.	Maharashtra	5063062	4818594	9881656	10.20
16.	Manipur	29934	30103	60037	2.77
17.	Meghalaya	5920	5219	11139	0.48
18.	Mizoram	212	60	272	0.03
19.	Nagaland	0	0	0	0.00
20.	Orissa	3073278	3008785	6082063	16.53
21.	Punjab	3714350	3314373	7028723	28.85
22.	Rajasthan	5067679	4626783	9644462	17.16
23.	Sikkim	13807	13358	27165	5.02
24.	Tamil Nadu	5932925	5924579	11857504	19.00
25.	Tripura	283186	272538	555724	17.37
26.	Uttar Pradesh	18502838	16645539	35148377	17.87
27.	Uttaranchal	780772	736414	1517186	21.15
28.	West Bengal	9469659	8982896	18452555	23.02
29.	Andaman and Nicobar Islands	0	0	0	0.00
30.	Chandigarh	86187	71410	157597	17.50
31.	Dadra and Nagar Haveli	2159	1945	4104	1.86
32.	Daman and Diu	2498	2340	4838	1.86

Source: Registrar General of India, Census of India 2001.

GEOGRAPHICAL BACKGROUND OF WEST BENGAL

West Bengal (Poshchim Bônggo) is a state in eastern India. With Bangladesh, which lies on its eastern border, the state forms the ethno-linguistic region of Bengal. To its northeast lie the states of Assam and Sikkim and the country Bhutan, and to its southwest, the state of Orissa. To the west it borders the state of Jharkhand and Bihar, and to the northwest, Nepal.

The name of Bengal, or Bangla, is derived from the ancient kingdom of Vanga, or Banga. References to it occur in early Sanskrit literature, but its early history is obscure until the 3rd century BC, when it formed part of the extensive Mauryan Empire inherited by Asoka. With the decline of Mauryan power, anarchy once more supervened. The history of Bengal (including Bangladesh and West Bengal) dates back four millennia. To some extent, the Ganga and the Brahmaputra rivers separated it from the mainland of India,

Remnants of Copper Age settlements in the Bengal region date back 4,000 years though at times, Bengal has played an important role in Indian history. Then the region was settled by Dravidian, Tibeto-Burman and Austro-Asiatic peoples. After the arrival of Indo-Aryans, the kingdoms of Anga, Vanga and Magadha were formed by the 10th century BC, located in and around the Bengal region. The Anga, Vanga and Magadha kingdoms are first described in the Atharvaveda around 1000 BC.

From the 6th century BC, most of Bengal was a part of the powerful kingdom of Magadha, which was an ancient Indo-Aryan kingdom of ancient India, mentioned in both the Ramayana and the Mahabharata. It was also one of the four main kingdoms of India at the time of Buddha, having risen to power during the reigns of Bimbisara (c. 544-491 BC) and his son Ajatashatru (c. 491-460 BC). Magadha spanned to include most of Bihar and Bengal. Magadha formed one of the sixteen Maha Janapadas (Sanskrit, "great country"). The Magadha Empire included republican communities such as Rajakumara. Villages had their own assemblies under their local chiefs called Gramakas. Their administrations were divided into executive, judicial, and military functions. Bimbisara was friendly to both Jainism and Buddhism and suspended tolls at the river ferries for all ascetics after the Buddha was once stopped at the Ganges River for lack of money.

In 326 BC, the army of Alexander the Great approached the boundaries of the Nanda Empire of Magadha. The army, exhausted and frightened by the prospect of facing a larger Indian army at the Ganges River, mutinied at the Hyphasis (modern Beas) and refused to march further east. Magadha was the seat of the Maurya Empire, founded by Chandragupta Maurya, which extended over nearly all of South Asia and parts of Persia and Afghanistan under Ashoka the Great; and later, of the powerful Gupta Empire, which extended over the northern Indian subcontinent and parts of Persia and Afghanistan.

One of the earliest foreign references to Bengal is the mention of a land named Gangaridai by the Greeks around 100 BC. The word is speculated to have come from Gangahrd (Land with the Ganges in its heart) and believed to be referring to an area in Bengal. For example, Diodorus Siculus (c. 90-30 BC) states that, ".Gandaridai, a nation which possesses the greatest number of elephants and the largest in size." This is presently known as 'Gangaridi' civilization and encompasses a period presumably from 400 BC to 100 AD. Some recent excavations in South 24 Parganas in West Bengal reveal small pearls of garnet, opal, quartz etc, which helped to detect the time and life-style of the people of this ancient civilization. There are engravings such as couple, snake, swastika, plough, trident, betel-leaf etc. found on these pearls.

PEOPLE OF WEST BENGAL

The peopling of West Bengal in pre-history is still to be reconstructed. The archaeologists have associated the Mundari speaking people with the use of copper hordes, rice cultivation, domestication of plants and animals. A DNA-based study establishes the speakers of the Austro-Asiatic languages as the oldest settlers in this region. It is speculated that the ancient peoples Vanga and Pundra were Austaloid (Chattopadyay, 2002). In Bengal there are place names to reconstruct the pattern of early settlements. In Bengal there are place names of Aryan, non-Aryan (Kol and Dravidian) and Tibeto Burman origin.

Bengal was a multi-ethnic region in the ancient period. There are references to many communities such as Vangas, Pundras, Sumas and Radhas, Gaudas and Gaudiyas, all named after the territories. There were two typical Bengali castes: Ambashta or Kayastha and Vaidya. The *Brihadharampuran* gives us the ethnic profile of Bengal before the Muslim conquest. This *puran* speaks of three groups of people, viz., (i) group of twenty good mixed castes (*uttam sankarah*), (ii) twelve *madyyama* or intermediate mixed castes, and (iii) eight *antyajas* or outcastes.

The partition of India in 1947 brought about a major shift in the ethnographic scenario of West Bengal, with the influx of mainly Hindu populations of all classes and castes including the Vaidya from East Pakistan, now Bangladesh.

There are 203 communities in the West Bengal under the project POI, as many as 140 communities constituting 70.0 per cent live in rural areas; 18 communities (8.9%) live in urban areas and about 38 communities (18.7%) inhabit rural/urban settings.

The major general communities of West Bengal and their approximate population according to the 1931 Census are as follows: Mahishya 20,75,840; Brahman 14,47; Kayastha/Karan/Prabhu 6,76,654; Sadgop 5,50,813; Tanti 3,10,805. However the census figure of the major scheduled castes as per 1981 census are Rajbanshi 22,58,760; Namasudra 16,92,233; Pod/Poundra 15,36,197; Bagdi 18,31,565; Chamar, Muchi etc. 7,11,024; Bauri 7,32,205; Jalia Kaiborta 3,18,344; Dhoba/Dhubi 2,51,737; Dom/Dhangad 2,31,595. The scheduled tribes are Santal 16,66,610; Oraon 4,37,574; Bhumij/Bhumiji 2,33,906; Munda 2,30,016.

Some of the indigenous communities of West Bengal include the Brahman, Kayastha/Karan/Prabhu, Mahishya, Bagdi, Rajbanshi and Namasudra, while the immigrant communities include the Bihari, Chinese Gujarati, and Jew/Bene Israel. The minorities in the state are Anglo-Indian, Bihari, Jew/Bene, Israel and Sikhs. The Lodha is a de-notified community while Anglo-Indian is a typical example of a miscegenated group.

According to the Census 2001 the total population in West Bengal is 801,76,197 and out of which scheduled caste population is 23.02 per cent i.e. (184,52,555).

SCHEDULED CASTES OF WEST BENGAL

Population of India can be divided broadly into three sections i.e. Scheduled Tribes, Scheduled Castes and Non-Scheduled Communities, though since few years past another section has been identified, known as Other Backward Classes. It is to be kept in mind that even before Independence; a list was prepared by identifying Castes and Tribes under a single schedule. Only in 1955 and 1956 two separate lists were published. The last Amendment Order of Scheduled Caste and Scheduled Tribe were issued in 1976. According to that Order, there are 59 Scheduled Castes in West Bengal.

The state West Bengal holds the third position having the large number of scheduled caste population in comparison to the state of India. The population of scheduled castes of West Bengal shares 23.62 per cent of the total SCs population in India. The caste history of West Bengal is very old. Before the Aryan influence, ancient Bengal was chiefly inhabited by the Austric and Dravida tribes. In some ancient Hindu, Jaina as well as Buddhist literatures like Aitareya Aranyaka, Mahabharata, Bhagavata Purana, Dharmasutra by Bodhayana, Acharanga-Ayaranga Sutra and Aryamanjusri Mula, etc., these tribes are referred as 'Dasyu', 'Mleccha', 'Papa' and 'Asura'. Their languages were as foreign and unintelligible to the Aryans as those of the birds. Introduction of castes system on the Aryan pattern did not start until the fifth century A.D. To be precise, the Gupta dynasty (300-550 A.D.) primarily patronized the stratification of Bengal society on Varna and jati lines. In the period of Pala dynasty (750-1135 A.D.), caste lower than the Brahmin were prominent. The Brahmanical order was reinforced at the close of the Pala dynasty through the ideological stewardship of a Brahmin scholar named Bhavadev Bhatta. But it was the Sena kings of Bengal (1095-1205 A.D.), among whom Bhilla Sena (1158-1179 A.D.) and Lakshman Sena (1179-1205 A.D.) are to be named separately, who tried their utmost to Aryanise the entire Bengal society against the pre-dominant tribal and non-Aryan influences. They elaborated the code of conduct for every caste and sub-caste and made strict rules for their application and declared those elements patit (degenerate) with whom they came into conflict as a social group.

Historically, Bengal can claim at least two special features in regard to caste. First, there was only one Dvija caste, which was the Brahmin. The other two Dvija castes, namely, Kshatriya and Vaisya hardly existed in Bengal. Other than the Brahmins, all the castes in Bengal originated from large-scale mixing of local people and tribes. Those castes were mentioned to in the early writings as "Sankara". Thus, the caste structure in Bengal was divided into four broad layers. At the apex, there were Brahmins, below them in the hierarchy were placed the upper Sudras (referred to as Uttam Sankara" in the Brahaddhama Purana and as "Sat Sudra" in the Brahmavaivarta Purana), then the lower Sudras, i.e., "Madhyam Sankara" and "Patit" or "Asat Sudra", respectively. Below these castes were the untouchables ("Antyaje" or "Adhama Sankara"). The Melecchas and some tribes from within and outside Bengal were kept out of the caste society. The untouchables groups later on considered as scheduled caste after 1935, just after Simon Commission declared them as scheduled caste. In this way caste system came into being into the West Bengal. At present there are fifty nine (59) communities have been recognized as scheduled caste in West Bengal. According to the Census report 1991 the total SCs population in West Bengal was 1,60,80,611 and in 2001, 1,84,52,555. Distribution of population among different communities of scheduled caste is shown in Table 2.2.

In the state, out of fifty nine communities of scheduled caste four communities (Rajbanshi, Namasudra, Pod or Poundra and Bagdi) constitute 62.61 per cent of the total scheduled caste population in West Bengal.

Table 2.2: Distribution of Population of Different Communities among Scheduled Castes according to Census 1981-2001 of India, West Bengal

Name of the Castes	*1981*	*1991*	*2001*
All Scheduled Castes	100.00	100.00	100.00
1. Bagdi, Duley	15.26	14.64	14.85
2. Bahelia	0.04	0.04	0.02
3. Baiti	0.08	0.09	0.06
4. Bantar	0.02	0.03	0.00
5. Bauri	6.10	5.91	5.91
6. Beldar	0.02	0.02	0.02
7. Bhogta	0.12	0.10	0.08
8. Bhuimali	0.40	0.42	0.43
9. Bhuiya	0.78	0.74	0.68
10. Bind	0.28	0.28	0.28
11. Chamar	5.92	5.74	5.39
12. Chaupal	0.02	0.05	0.03
13. Dabgar	Ng.	0.00	0.00
14. Damai (Nepali)	0.16	0.14	0.09
15. Dhoba, Dhobi	2.10	2.11	2.00
16. Doai	0.07	0.06	0.02
17. Dom, Dhangad	1.93	1.76	1.71
18. Dosadh, Dusadh, Dhari, Dharhi	0.33	0.34	0.33
19. Ghasi	0.15	0.13	0.08
20. Gonrhi	0.12	0.15	0.10
21. Halalkhor	0.01	0.01	0.00
22. Hari, Mehtar, Mehtor, Bhangi	2.23	2.24	2.11
23. Jalia Kaibartta	2.65	2.75	2.21
24. Jhalo Malo, Malo	1.29	1.37	1.59
25. Kadar	0.08	0.09	0.13
26. Kami (Nepali)	0.35	0.34	0.26
27. Kandra	0.54	0.49	0.50
28. Kanjar	0.01	0.01	0.00
29. Kaora	1.51	1.55	1.42
30. Karenga, Koranga	0.18	0.16	0.18
31. Kaur	0.17	0.14	0.06
32. Keot, Keyot	0.38	0.37	0.04
33. Khaira	0.65	0.55	0.06
34. Khatik	0.04	0.07	0.04
35. Koch	0.08	0.09	0.06
36. Konai	0.06	0.55	0.58
37. Konwar	0.02	0.03	0.02
38. Kotal	0.16	0.14	0.13
39. Kurariar	0.01	0.00	0.00
40. Lalbegi	0.01	0.00	0.00
41. Lohar	1.26	1.36	1.56
42. Mahar	0.15	0.14	0.15
43. Mal	1.71	1.43	1.48
44. Mallah	0.32	0.30	0.27

(Contd.)

Name of the Castes	1981	1991	2001
45. Musahar	0.15	0.14	0.12
46. Namasudra	14.10	16.05	17.40
47. Nat	0.03	0.02	0.00
48. Nuniya	0.35	0.30	0.30
49. Paliya	0.97	0.83	0.70
50. Pan, Sawasi	0.08	0.09	0.12
51. Pasi	0.18	0.17	0.13
52. Patni	0.19	0.18	0.16
53. Pod, Poundra	12.80	12.34	12.01
54. Rajbanshi	18.82	17.65	18.35
55. Rajwar	0.71	0.68	0.53
56. Sarki (Nepali)	0.09	0.10	0.06
57. Sunri (ExcludingSaha	2.10	2.05	1.72
58. Tiyar	0.68	0.99	1.05
59. Turi	0.24	0.24	0.20
60. Unclassified	0.21	0.94	1.00

Source: Census of India, West Bengal 1981, 1991 and 2001.

In all the districts of West Bengal comprises scheduled castes population with its general population in various proportions. Out of which South 24 Paragana (12.02%), Burdhwan (10.08%), North 24 Paragana (9.97%), Medinipur (8.54%), Jalpaiguri (6.76%), and Kóch Bihar (6.73%) comprise more fifty percent i.e. (54.1%) (According to Census of India 2001) scheduled castes population of the state. In the following Table 2.3 distribution of scheduled castes population in different districts of West Bengal from 1951-2001 is shown.

ETHNOGRAPHICAL DESCRIPTION ABOUT THE SCHEDULED CASTE OF WEST BENGAL

As it is mentioned earlier that, there are fifty nine (59) sub-communities are considered as scheduled castes in West Bengal. Out of these 59 communities the major 10 sub-communities are—Namasudra (17.40), Rajbanshi (18.35), Bagdi, Duley (14.85), Pod, Poundra (12.01), Barui (5.91), Chamar (5.39), Jalia Kaiborta (2.21), Hari, Mehtar, Mehtor, Bhangi (2.11) Dhoba, Dhobi (2.00) and Jhalo Malo (1.59) constitute (81.82%) of the total scheduled castes of the state. The remaining forty nine scheduled castes cover the rest of the population.

Among the Scheduled Castes Baruis and Sunris are distributed mainly in the districts of Banker, Birbhum, Hugli, Bardhawan, Puruliya, Medinipur, Haora and 24 Parganas. The Chamars are mostly migrants of Bihar and they are distributed throughout the state of West Bengal. The

Table 2.3: District-Wise Distribution on Scheduled Caste Population of West Bengal from 1951-2001

Sl. No.	*State/Districts*	*1951*	*1961*	*1971*	*1981*	*1991*	*2001*
1.	West Bengal	18.93	19.73	19.90	21.99	23.62	23.00
2.	Koch Bihar	40.15	46.90	47.03	49.85	51.76	50.13
3.	Jalpaiguri	25.72	30.80	34.02	34.61	36.99	36.68
4.	Darjeeling	5.86	13.19	12.57	14.25	16.15	16.12
5.	Uttar Dinajpur	17.09	21.64	23.10	28.57	28.96	27.70
6.	Daxin Dinajpur	–	–	–	–	29.10	28.79
7.	Maldah	14.54	13.38	16.48	16.89	18.12	16.84
8.	Murshidabad	11.64	12.32	12.27	13.05	13.40	12.00
9.	Nadia	16.72	20.44	21.20	26.21	29.01	29.67
10.	North24 Paragana	22.86	24.28	22.61	25.04	21.49	20.60
11.	South24 Paragana	–	–	–	–	24.45	32.10
12.	Kolkata	4.85	4.33	3.78	4.54	6.45	06.00
13.	Haora	13.76	14.71	12.31	15.29	15.79	15.41
14.	Hugli	20.59	18.95	19.08	21.58	24.12	23.58
15.	Medinipur	14.37	12.98	13.57	14.60	16.64	16.35
16.	Banker	31.19	29.60	28.22	28.90	31.36	31.24
17.	Puruliya	–	14.77	14.99	18.78	19.25	18.30
18.	Burdhwan	26.68	24.45	24.51	25.09	27.44	26.89
19.	Birbhum	29.77	29.14	30.00	29.80	30.68	29.53
20.	Chandernagar	10.93	–	–	–	–	–

Source: (i) *Bulletin of the Cultural Research Institute,* Vol. XIX, No. 3.
(ii) Census of India, West Bengal 2001.

main concentration of the Namasudra, Poundra is noticed in the districts of Nadia, 24 Parganas, Haris and Doms are present in all over the state. The Jalia Kaibortas are the fisher folk of Bengal and have made their habitations in the districts of Maldah, Murshidabad and to a greater number is also distributed along the coastal areas of 24 Parganas, Medinipur and Haora. The Damais are distributed in the Darjeeling districts. The Koch and Rajbanshis are mainly noticed in the districts of Jalpaiguri, KochBihar and in some coastal areas of 24-Parganas, Haora and Medinipur. All the sub communities of the scheduled castes of West Bengal are having separate history of its origin and have living style, which is quite necessary to know to have clear idea about the scheduled castes of West Bengal. A brief description about 10 major sub-communities of scheduled castes of West Bengal are narrated below—

Rajbanshi: The Rajbanshis are a cultivating and landowning community of North Bengal. They are also known as Desi or Bahey and Rajbanshi Kshattriya. Sanyal (1965) says that 'the history of the origin of the Rajbanshi is a mystery. It is said that they belong to the great Bodo family that entered India in the 10tj century B.C., from the east and settled on the banks of the Brahmaputra and gradually spread over Assam and the whole of North Bengal'. Risley describes that Koch, Koch-Mandi, Rajbanshi, Palliya, and Desi belong to a large Dravidian tribe of north eastern and eastern Bengal amongst whom there are grounds for suspecting some admixture of Mongolian blood. The transformation of Koch into Rajbanshi, the name by which they are now known in Jalpaiguri, Koch Bihar, is a singular illustration of the influence exercised by fiction in the making of caste. Now the great majority of Koch inhabitants of northern Bengal invariably describe themselves as Rajbanshis or Bhanga Kshatriyas. They are thoroughly Koch under the name Rajbanshi. There is no historical foundation for claim of Rajbanshis to be a provincial variety of Kshatriyas. (Risley, 1891:1:491). Rajbanshis are belong to scheduled caste community, and they are the largest group of scheduled caste in West Bengal, which shares (18.35%), (According to census 2001) to the total scheduled caste in West Bengal. The Rajbanshis are mainly noticed in the district of Jalpaiguri, Koch Bihar and in some coastal areas of 24-Parganas, Haora and Medinipur. Rajbanshis had their relations with the great Bodo Kachari group of Assam. The literacy rate of this group of people is 60.14 per cent in 2001 and in 1991 it was 40.71 per cent.

Namasudra: The second largest scheduled caste of West Bengal is Namasudra; they share 17.40 per cent to the total scheduled caste of the state. Namasudras are the indigenous group people of the state. Namasudra is a scheduled caste community found in Bengal and especially in East-Bengal (present Bangladesh) wherever there are rivers and canals. They lived crammed into villages divided by canals, creeks and streams, reached by rowing boat, by hand-poled ferries, by rope, log or bamboo bridges swaying dangerously over the rushing waters which poured through the region. "The Namasudras are not inconsiderable in number in the districts like Faridpur, Bakherganj, Khulna and Jessore, there are large areas with extensive Namausdra settlements" (Bose: 1975:158).

The term Namasudra is seldom found in any authentic Sanskrit Literature. But this term is found mentioning in Shyamcharan Sarkar's Vyasnastha Darpan as a subdivision of Sudra caste (Lahiri & Dev: 1982: 155). And etymologically this term means a group of respected Sudra. Namah,—names respected, and Sudra, is a classified section of people who holds the lower strata in the caste society. Besides this many other writers have narrated about the origin of Namasudra in Indian society which has been narrated in the part *Evolution of Namasudra* in this chapter. The Namasudras are a traditional agricultural community. Besides agriculture, navigating boat is also a traditional occupation among them. They are the follower of Sam Veda. They observe all the existing religious festivals in the year like other caste group. They engage Brahmin in all worship such as puja, marriage ceremony and other social functions. In Sardha ceremony, they pay homage to their forefather on the 10tj day after death. They are permitted to offer rice panda (funeral cake) in Gaya Pitha. It may be added here that "The Brahmin that served them were classed as a degraded Brahmin group" (Ghurya: 1969:317).

Namasudra is sub-divided into three groups according to their place of original inhabitations of the past. These sub-divisions are Shiuli, Sandipi and Vikrampuri. The group Shiuli was inhabitant of Shiuli-Chatal, i.e. the area of Gopalganj and Madaripiur of district Faridpur (Bala: Bengali Year 1980:8). Similarly, the group Sandipi was the inhabitant of Sandipi area, i.e. Khula district and its surrounding areas. (*ibid*: 31) and the group Vikrampuri was the inhabitant of Vikrampur, i.e. present Vikrampur and Idalpur of Daka (Roy: 145). In West Bengal, according to census 1872 their number was 201,745, in 1901 their number was 174,888 in 1951, 324,723. At present their number according to census 1991 was 25,81,549 and in 2001, their population is 32,12,393. Namasudra in West Bengal, academically sound than the other communities of scheduled caste. The literacy rate of Namasudra people 1n 1991 census of India was 56.18 per cent and in the census 2001 of India are 71.93. They are mostly concentrated in the districts of Nadia, 24-Parganas, Jalpaiguri, Koch Bihar etc.

Bagdi, Duley: Bagdi, Bagtit, Mudi a cultivating, fishing, and menial caste of central and Western Bengal, who appear from their features and complexion to be of Dravidian descent, and closely akin to the tribes whom, for convenience of description, we may call aboriginal. Referring to the Brahmavaibarta Purana, Mitra (1953), states that the Bagdi are the descendents of a union between a Kshatriya father and a Vaishya mother. They are notified as Bagdi, Duley in West Bengal, and they are considered as the scheduled caste of the state. Bagdi are spreaded all over the state. According to the census report of India 1981, their total population was 1,831,565,, in 1991, 23,54,609 and in 2001 their total population is 2,740,385. Their educational development may be inferring form their literacy rate from various census reports. Literacy rate of this groups are 13.96 per cent (census, 1981), 30.02 per cent (census, 1991) and 47.72 per cent (census, 2001).

Pod, Poundra: Poundra Kshtariya is one of the major scheduled caste communities in the state of West Bengal. From the very beginning (1931) the community was included in the list of Depressed Classes and later on (1936) as scheduled caste. This caste also known as 'Pod' and they called themselves as Padmaraja too. Regarding the origin of this community, observation of T.C. Roy Chowdhary (39 ISCP 1952) may be referred wherein he stated that "from the time of Brahmin and Smriti dawn to the time of Hiuen Tsang, a group of powerful people named Poundra lived in the Western part of Bengal and that they were of non-Aryan origin i.e. Pre-Dravidian. He further stated that 'the Pods of modern days are the descendant of the ancient Paundras'. Mr. H. Beverly (census 1872) has also indicated that 'the name, Pod derived from Paundra, who were ancient people inhabiting in lower Bengal from Munger to Jessore in the age of Mahabharat and that Paundras were an aboriginal people and the Pod a remnant of the ancient people'. However, from the reports of the Ethnographers it is still difficult to come to a conclusion whether the Pods or the Punros represent ancient Pundras or Poundras a well known Kshatriya tribe. Pods or Poundras are the dominant scheduled caste group in West Bengal, their total population was 15,36,197 (Census, 1981), 19,85,243 Census, 1991 and 22,16,513 (Census, 2001), which is 12.80 per cent, 12.34 per cent and 12.01 per cent respectively of the total scheduled caste population in the state.

In the field of education, this community made a definite progress, which may be marked from different census reports. Literacy rate of this community was 36.49 per cent in census, 1981, 56.05 per cent in census, 1991 and 72.10 per cent in census, 2001.

Barui: "Barai" the names of the two castes engaged in Bengal and Behar, respectively, in the cultivation of piper betel, ordinarily known as pan (Sansk.parna), the leaf par excellence. Although their occupation is the same, provincial and linguistic distinctions separate the Bengali speaking Barui of Bengal and the Hindi-speaking Barai of Behar into two entirely distinct castes, who do not intermarry or eat together, and whose domestic usages differ in important particulars. Barui use such titles as Majumdar, Haldar, Khan, Sarkar, Bardhan etc. Risley (1988) noted that the Baruis are divided into four endogamous sub-castes: (i) Barhi, (ii) Barendra, (iii) Nathan, and (iv) Kota.

They claim they are a clean caste belonging to the *nabasakha* group, and this is corroborated by Risley's works. All informants say they are the autochthons of the areas where they live now. Baruis are distributed throughout West Bengal. Their total population in West Bengal was 7,32,205 in census, 1981, 9,50,692 in census, 1991 and 10,91,022 in census, 2001. Their development in the field of education may be observed from different census report of India. Their literacy rate was 9.42 per cent in census, 1981, 21.47 per cent in census, 1991 and 37.46 per cent in census, 2001. So, from the table it is found that their academic progress is growing day by day.

Chamar Charmakar, Mochi, Muchi, Rabidas, Ruidas, and Rishi: Chamar is another major sub-community of scheduled caste of West Bengal. The Chamar is one of the major communities found in almost all the states of northern India as well as in other regions. Their community name is derived from the Sanskrit word charmakara, meaning leather worker. Risley (1891) writes that, according to the Puranas, the Chamars descended from the union of a boatman and a Chandal woman. But scholars identify them with the Karewara or leather worker mentioned in the tenth chapter of Manu's Dharmashutra. The father of the caste was a Nishada and the mother Vaidcha. Chamar community is found in all the districts of West Bengal. The Chamars are mostly migrants of Bihar and they distributed throughout the state of West Bengal. The Chamar holds the sixth position in the population rank with 5.39 per cent to the total scheduled caste population in West Bengal according to census 2001 of India. At present their population is 9,95,756 and in 1991 census of India was 9,24,547 and in 1981, 7,11,024. Their literacy rate from various census of India shows the progress in the field of education in the state. Their literacy rate is 14.42 per cent (Census, 1981), 28.08 per cent (Census, 1991) and 46.99 per cent (Census).

Jalia Kaiborta: Jalia Kaiborta, this is another scheduled caste group of West Bengal which constitutes 2.21 per cent (Census, 2001) to the total scheduled caste population of West Bengal. In the Census 1981 of India their total population was 3,18,344 and in 1991, 4,42,783 and in 2001 Census of India their total population is 4,09,303; which is 2.65 per cent, 2.75 per cent and 2.21 per cent to the total scheduled caste population in West Bengal according to the Census report 1981, 1991 and 2001 respectively. Risley (1891) states Kaibarta-Das, Chasi-Das, Halia-Das, Parasar-das, Dhivara, Khyan, a large fishing and cultivating caste of Bengal Proper, taking rank below the Nava-sakha, or group of nine castes, from whose hands a Brahmin may take water. No serious attempt can be made to trace the origin of the Kaibarta. The Physical character of the caste are not marked enough to throw any certain light on their descent, while their exogamous divisions, having been obviously borrowed from the Brahmins, contribute in no way to the solution of the question. The Jalia Kaibartas are the fisher-folk of Bengal and have made their inhabitations in the districts of Maldah, Murshidabad and to a greater number is also distributed along the coastal areas of 24-Paraganas, Medinipur and Haora. Educationally also they are not backward too much than the other community of West Bengal. Their academic progress may observe from the literacy rate from the various Census report of West Bengal. Their literacy rate in the Census 1981 of India was 30.16 per cent, in 1991, 49.31 and in 2001 Census of India is 64.85 per cent which is more than the all scheduled caste literacy rate in West Bengal.

Hari, Mehtar, Mehtor, Bhangi: Hari, Mehtar, Mehtor, Bhangi constitutes 2.11 per cent of the total scheduled caste population in West Bengal. Hari also known as Hadi or Haddi, they were traditionally engaged in collecting the earthen pots used in burial grounds for death rituals. Hari means an earthen pot used for death rituals. They are migrants group of West Bengal; they have migrated from the states Uttar Pradesh, Andhra Pradesh, Rajasthan, Maharashtra, Gujarat and Orissa. Mehtar, meaning a prince or a leader, is an ironic title given to the people who are traditionally engaged as sweepers and scavengers and are known by different names in different parts of the country, like Bhangi, Hari, Mehtor Lalbegi and so on. In West Bengal they are also playing dominant role in making the scheduled caste group larger. According to the Census 1981, their population, including all the above mentioned name, in West Bengal was 267,465, in 1991, 3,60,736 and in 2001 Census, their population is 390,619. Their present literacy rate is 49.45 per cent (Census, 2001) and in 1991 their literacy rate was 42.10 per cent.

Jhalo Malo: Jhalo Malo is the fishing community of the West Bengal, Assam, Tripura and other North-Eastern states. They are belonging to Scheduled caste community in all the above mentioned states. As their main profession is fishing, so, they are preferred to live near by the river bank of the state West Bengal and other states. The word Jhalo Malo comprise the two words, Jhalo and Malo; the former may be the corrupt form of the word jaal meaning net or jal meaning water, and the later may be a derivative of the Arabic word mallah, which means boatman. They are predominantly rural based. However, a good number of them are returned from urban areas. The Indo-Aryan language, Bengali, and the Bengali script are used for both inter and intra group communication. According to the Census 2001 of India their population in West Bengal is 2,93,714, which 1.59 per cent of the total scheduled caste population of the state. In the field of education they are also growing very fast; in this regard their literacy rate may be brought into light. According to Census 1981 of India their literacy rate was 25.51 per cent, but in 1991 their position stood up to 42.52 per cent and in the Census 2001, their position became 60.33, which better than the all scheduled caste population in the state.

Dhoba, Dhobi: This is another group of scheduled caste in West Bengal which constitutes 2.00 per cent to the total scheduled caste of the state. In West Bengal they are known as Dhopa, Dhobi and Rajak, and the latter is in fact used as a title. A reference to the origin of the Dhobas can be found in the *Skanda* and Brahma *Vaibarta Puranas.* They are distributed all over the state west Bengal. Their traditional occupation is washing clothes. According to the Census report 1981 their total population was 2,51,737 which is 2.10 per cent to the total scheduled caste population of the state. In the Census 1991 of India their population was 3,39,555 which is 2.11 per cent and in 2001, 3,69,808 and which is 2 per cent of the total population. The Dhobas are academically very sound, which may be proved from their literacy rate from the various census reports. Their literacy rate was 38.79 per cent in (census, 1981), 62.07 per cent in (Census, 1991) and in 2001, 73.87 per cent which far better than the other communities of scheduled caste of West Bengal. So, from the Census report it is found that they academically so sound, which is far above than the national level literacy rate. Presently, maximum of them preferred to live in the urban areas, which helps them to get education.

EVOLUTIONARY ASPECT OF NAMASUDRA

History is the witness of the past; the real cast odium of evidences, helping the near and far future for its smooth functioning. In the process of evolution or during the causation of a certain revolution, how a particular nation or tribe establishes their self identity and self stability dedicating even thousands of lives, how crooked effect of particular dynasty emotionalizes the developmental shifting of a certain section or group of people inducing the sentiment of disintegration communal disharmony. The history carries all the silent pathetic documentary records, thereby assisting the conscious mass through a thorough enquiry in the ratification and outbreak of new ideas, concepts, theories and strategies.

The concept of evolution indicates a slow gradual process of adoption and suitable transformation to up with the prevailing unfavourable situation or environment, resulting in a new status or position or structure, similar to some extent with the earliest one. Due to the mighty influence of certain dynasty, as we see in the ancient Indian history, a particular tribe or community sacrifices the different attributes of life, even the life itself suppressing the earnest demand and real identity only to save them from the havoc of destruction. Yes, the same sadistic episode with full of authoritarian negligence cruel command and injustice was observed in the case history of 'Namasudra community' who were treated badly by the mighty influence of the then Bengal lord named Ballal Sen.

The etymology of the word 'Namasudra' which is not mentioned in any of the pre-nineteenth century Medieval Bengali literature, is extremely, uncertain colonial ethnologists like James Wise and Herbert Risely believed that it was derived either from the Sanskrit word 'namas' or adoration or the Bengali word 'namate' i.e. below or underneath. In the first case it would mean those who were bound to show obeisance even to the Shudras. In the second case, the word would perhaps mean a lower grade of Shudras, a status the Chandalas of Manu had gained promotion to. But these two explanations appear to be highly improbable in view of the new sense of self respect associated with the Namasudra identity. The Namasudras themselves were also confused about the meaning of the term. Sashi Kumar Badoi Biswas thought that the word could mean two things: namaskar or paying obeisance to and tyaja or to be avoided. If the word was used in the first sense, then it would mean those who paid obeisance to the Shudras (Shudrang namati). But had it been in the second sense, then it would mean avoided by Shudras (Namah Shudrena). None of the meanings, however, seemed to be acceptable to him, though he had failed to arrive at definite conclusion. According to another Namasudra commentator, Naresh Chandra Das, the word means the Shudras who were paid obeisance to an explanation which seems to be the most plausible of all.

The different synonymous of the Namasudras are Chandal, Charal, Namasud and Namah. In the census of 1901, at which caste names and caste precedence were scrutinized and registered rather minutely, the Chandalas of Bengal, who were otherwise known as Namasudras Though the Namasudra people were considered as Chandal in earlier text of India, but that can't be absolutely accepted. Because it is only Ballal Sen did and then lord of Bengal considered the Namasudra people as Chandal and untouchable.

There should be a separate history for the Namasudra people so far as their evolutionary concept is concerned. Ballal Sen then the lord of Bengal who wanted to abolish the word Namasudra from the Indian history and forcefully he made them Chandal and he ordered other people also to consider Namasudra people as Chandal during his tenure.

If we analyze different religious scripts and "Jatitattwa" books of India then we will find that the Namasudras are neither Chandal nor Shudra rather they are the Brahmin offspring. As we have know that during the

Aryan period due to the process of Aryanisation and Non-Aryanisation Shudra people evolved. In other way the Shudra people were considered very lower during that period as because they were born out from the feet of the lord or Creator of the all creatures. Chandal is who according to the scripture a progeny of illegitimate liaisons between Brahmin female and a Shudra male. During that period a higher caste people could marry a lower caste people and that was accepted in their society after purification; but the vise-versa could not accepted and their offspring were referred as Chandal and they were considered as untouchable later. So, we find that Chandals are the offspring of Shudra male and Brahmin female. But the history of Namasudra is different; they are not offspring of Shudra male and Brahmin female rather they are the offspring of Brahmin male and Shudra female.

Namasudra in Texts

The term Namasudra is seldom found in any authentic Sanskrit literature. But this term is found mentioning in Shymacharan Sarkar's Vyasnastha Darpan as a sub-division of Sudra caste (Lahiri and Dev: 1982:155). And etymologically this term means a group of respected Sudra. Naman,— names respected, and Sudra, is a classified section of people who holds the lower strata in the caste society.

According to 'Namasudra suhrid' by Raicharan Biswas (January, 1908), "We are of the Brahmin Caste; perhaps because of anger or of envy many may be unable to like us, but observing our Brahmanical conduct through the ages, everyone agrees unanimously that the Namasudra caste is descended from the ancient sages, i.e. from the purest Brahmins. The second point is that our source of livelihood is the Aryan practice of agriculture, that glorious occupation of ancient and modern times (Bose: 1975: 158). A similar view has been expressed in a book entitled 'Jattitatva O Namasya Kuladarpan' (*Ibid*).

According to Tarak Chandra Sarkar, "The Namasudras are the banished Brahman Buddhists who do not want to change their religion at the time of King Ballal Sen" (Sarkar: Bengali Year 1370:26).

In his book entitled *'Namasudra Dijatattva'* Pandit Rajbihari Roy Sarnakar hints that "The Namasudras are Brahmin. They were invited by the King Ballal Sen to preside over his marriage ceremony, but they refused to accept the post of priest in an inter-caste (Hypergamy) marriage, as because the would-be-wife was a Dom caste girl. Her name was Padmini. Ballal Sen ordered his soldier to kill this rebellion group and he declared this group as Sudra. (Das: Bengali Year, 1368:70). Sri Gostha

Bihari Debnath, a Nath teacher and scholar, in his Bengali works on Nathaism mentioned "The Namasudra have been given the position of Parasava Vipras" (Battacharyya): 1975: 157). They identify themselves as one of the superior groups, claiming their descent from the purest Brahmin origin. But "Hindu society has always despised this agricultural caste (Bose: 175: 157).

Namasudras are not Shudra which has been narrated by the different writers such as—Shri Gourpriya Sarkar in his book "Jatitattwa Sangraha" (Bengali), Shri Jitedranath Majumdar in his book "Jatitattwa and Namasudra Jatir Utpatti" "(Bengali), Shri Jogredra Chandra Majumdar in his book "Namasudra Jati Tattwa Katha" (Bengali), Shri Sattya Ranjan Sarkar in "Namasudra Jatitatttwa" "(Bengali), Shri Sukumar Sarkar in "Namasudrai Parsav Bipra" (Bengali), Shri Darakanath Mandal in "Namasudra Jatikatha" (Bengali) by referring different quotations from various religious books and by putting some example.

In the above mentioned books the authors have placed that Namasudras are neither Shudra nor Chandal rather they are Brahmin offspring by birth; but because of some social imposed force they lost their identity as Brahmin and as a result they had to live like a Shudra for their survival. The evolutionary history of Namasudra may be narrated in the following ways—

The Namasudra is a very strong group in comparison to the other caste in Bengal. But nowhere of the Indian scripts have mentioned the term Namasudra including Veda and other religious books in present society. But the question is why it happened and what the reason behind of this is. In the oldest religious book of Hindu just mentioned about four group of people such as—Brahmin, Ksahtriya, Vaishya and Shudra but not about the Namasudra. Then what is the position of Namasudra and in which category they are belonging to? Or, how they have evolved in this world? After a long investigation one book named "Saktisangam Tantra" (in Sanskrit) was found in Bengal and there the evolution of Namasudra was narrated. In that book there is chapter named 'Prantoshi' where Lord Shiva narrated the story about Namasudra to goddess Parvati through conversation. In that book it has been narrated that the great saint 'Namash' was the son of saint 'Kashyapa' whose father was lord "Brahma's" son 'Marichi'. When the wife of saint Namash, Solochana was pregnant then he left home for tapsya for a long time. When he returned home after 14 years then he found that his wife has gave birth of two sons named 'Kirttiban' and 'Kuruban'. But his wife Solochana expired just after of her delivery and they were looked after and brought up by two saint

'Afshar' and 'Naidhruba'. After his arrival the saint 'Namash' was very much satisfied with his two sons and he wanted to make them purify by giving sacred thread as it is the ritual of Brahmin. But he couldn't make them purify as because they crossed their age limit 12 years. Then the saint 'Namash' again left home for a long time for his son's up gradation in the society. After a long wait Kirtiban and Kuruban left home for searching their father and finally they reached to a king named 'Simanta' at present Siliguri. The king Simanta was Sudra king and he had no son but, he had two daughter named 'Shipika' and 'Shapitraka'. Then the king made them agree to marry with his two daughters; and they got married with those two girls though they were Sudra by birth. In the course time Kirtiban and Kuruban produced number of children, later on these group of people were known as Namasudra. The word 'Namasudra' had its two parts i.e. 'namah' and 'sudra'; these two parts has been borrowed from the memory of their fore father saint 'Namash' and mother 'Shudra'. Actually the name of Namasudra was given by Lord 'Narayana'; when saint Namash succeeded from his tapsya then Lord Narayana gave him three boons, he was very much satisfied with his prayer. The three boons were—i) that though your sons married with Shudra girls still your generation will be equal to a Brahmin, ii) that your generation will be known by your name i.e. they will be known as Namasudra and iii) your name will be immortal. From that day onward the word Namasudra evolved and these group people also evolved.

The Namasudra people are Brahmin origin which may be accepted from the cultural point of view also. In Manu's Doshakosh Pangika it is mentioned that—

> *Namasudra jatakhyata sampradaya samvedadhikari!*
> Dashadishabadhya souchya palanang purusanakramena arjhyrate!
> Tirthe pravashe grehavashe cha sraddhadi karjhya!
> *Tena pakkanna pindadang bidhi drishyte*!!

It is also known from the 'Ballal Charit' that for the sake of a personal promise given to a Dum girl named Padmini to be married, the Bengal emperor Ballal Sen was obligated to invite the Kashypiya Brahmans to attend and participate in the midday meal party on the very day of engagement ceremony with the girl. But as a result of refusal of the invitation, the armed forces of the king were directed to tear off the 'Holi Brahmin Thread' through force and dexterity. Accordingly the Kashyapiya Brahmins of 'Mulghar were tortured highly physically as well as mentally.

These deprived Brahmins were later on entitled as 'Namasudra' during the time and took the shelter in East, West, South and North Bengal and also in the place of Andaman Nicobar Islands from their Mulghar (presently Josohar in Bangladesh) residential area. During the period of 1158-1179 (Ballal Sen dynasty) the 'Namasudra' of Bengal were deprived and neglected in all terms due to the continuation of ill effect of Sen Times. During that period Ballal Sen conferred the name Chandal in place of Namasudra and Brahmin and he abolished the name Namasudra from all kind of known religious book forcefully; and he made a rule that those who will not consider Namasudra as Chandal they will be suspended from job and they will be physically punished.

In this way the other caste people considered Namasudra people as Chandal and they started to loss their power, fame, right, property, education etc. and in course of time they were considered as untouchable like other Sudras in Bengal.

During the British period also Namasudra people were considered as Chandal or Charal; which the Namasudra people opposed and started agitation against so called higher caste people. The year of 1872 was a very important in India. Before 1872 some states and some districts were sending annual census statistics. The British Govt. however undertook first of all India census in 1872. This census recorded every caste and tribe of India. The govt. as a matter of policy went by the advice of the pundits regarding caste determination. It is worthwhile to mention that classification of castes and tribes by district magistrates were generally impartial, while the pundits and the native officials often failed to overcome caste prejudices and their enumeration cannot be considered objective. Sometimes they misled the census commissioner. It goes to the credit of the district magistrate, they on many occasions differed from the native census officers. Even British census executives were presumably influenced by the native officers. The striking indigenous Bangas (Namasudra) the most memories people of East Bengal nerve accepted the slang 'Chandal' which the Aryan brought it from Aryandom and slapped on them. This tribes were formerly dominant and it only because they lost their political supremacy and have fallen under the Yoke of the Brahmanas, that they have sunk to their present position.

The Chandal agitated for over thirty years for change of the nomenclature which was turned down by the authorities repeated on the advice of the pundits. Since 1901, they made more organized and determined attempts in this behalf. It is interesting to note that during (1911-1931) most castes of Bengal including Baidhyas and Kayasthas demanded change of caste nomenclature. In 1911, the total weight of the voluminous representation to the government was over 1 ½ mounds. The relation between the Chandals and the high caste Hindu was so strained and ill feeling ran so high that in 1911 they represented to the British Govt. for grant of treatment of the caste at per with the Muslims and demanded separate privileges.

Awakening among the Namasudra

The Namasudras were, predicting, batter against the 'Bhadralok' who were their social tormentors. It was against the social humiliation and persecution that the Namasudras observed a 'general strike' in 1873 in the district of Faridpur (presently in Bangladesh). And this is the country's first general strike. The report of C A. Kelly, ICS, District magistrate, Faridpur in this behalf discloses thus.

"In the early part of this year (1873) the Chandals made a general strike in the District of Faridpur (presently in Bangladesh) resolving not to serve anybody of the upper class, in whatever capacity, unless a better position among the Hindu caste than what they at present occupy was given to them".

Since 1880s the efforts of the Chandals to change their nomenclature to Namasudra are noticed. F.B. Peacock, commissioner, Presidency Division writes in a letter [No. 87 dated Alipur, the 18 July, 1881] that "The improvement in the conditions of the Chandals who are in the chief agriculturists in Narail sub-division [of Jessore District] has led them....to aspire to a superior status in the Hindu caste system. They called themselves Namasudra and profess to be Baishnab. W.C. Macpherson, ICS, Assistant commissioner, communicated the order of the Deputy Commissioner, Syllet thus: "that Namasudra must always be written not as Chang or Chandal for all persons of the said caste that Deputy Commissioner has ordered that any person who does not write Namasudra shall be removed from employ. On a memorandum submitted to the chief Commissioner, Assam by some prominent social activists of Cachar district for change of caste name from Chandal to Namasudra, his secretary [letter No. 2195 dated 19tj August, 1885] says ".... the chief Commissioner sees no objection to person to call themselves Namasudra being designated as such in official documents. Nevertheless, their prayer for change of caste nomenclature from Chandal to Namasudra was not allowed due solely to opposition of the orthodox Hindus. In 1911 the Bengal govt. effected the change to Namasudra by a notification.

In this regard the revered Namasudra socio-religious leader of Faridpur G C Thakur may be mentioned. Gourchand Thakur fought against the so-called caste Hindu for changing their name as Namasudra instead of Chandal in 1893.

In the present chapter, theoretical frameworks have been discussed to present the theoretical background of the study. In this respect the researcher has rationalized the anthropological approach for educational research in the present context. So far the study content of the present research is concerned the researcher has tried to give the genesis of caste and scheduled caste in India. At the same time again, attempt have been made to give the evolutionary aspect of Namasudras a major sub-caste of scheduled caste mostly found in Assam and West Bengal. Again, a brief ethnographical description of each sub-caste of scheduled castes people in Assam and West Bengal with a view to their social status and educational status have been discussed in the present chapter. To find out the more rationality and justification of the present study, the researcher has gone through number of research studies which have been discussed in the foregoing chapter.

REFERENCES

Laha, S.S. and Bhuimali, A. (2007) Genesis of Scheduled Castes and Constitutional Safeguards for them, (Ed.) *Development of Scheduled Caste, Anil Bhuimali,* Serial Publications, New Delhi, pp. 160-161.

Das, A.K. (1987), Scheduled Castes and Scheduled Tribes: A Socio-Economic and Cultural Profile, *Bulletin of the Cultural Research Institute*, Vol. XVII, No. 1-2, West Bengal.

Chatterjee, S.K. (2000), *Educational Development of Scheduled Castes*, Gyan Publishing House, New Delhi, pp. 411-441.

Wikipedia, the free Encyclopedia.

www.mapsofindia.co m.

Singh, K.S. (2008), *People of India, West Bengal*, Seagull Books, Calcutta, p. XIII.

Ibid., p. XV.

Ibid., p. XVIII.

Ibid., p. XXVII.

Census of India 2001.

Ray, U.K. and Choudhari, M.K. (1997), Scheduled Castes of West Bengal: Situational Analysis, (Ed.), *Bulletin of the Cultural Research Institute,* Vol. XIX, No. 2, West Bengal, p. 1.

Ray, N.R. (1980), *Bengali Ithihas: Adi Parba*, Calcutta Niraksharata Durikaran Samiti, (3rd ed) Vol. I, pp. 256-257.

Ibid., pp. 259-267, 308.
Ibid., pp. 267-278.
Ibid., pp. 249-250, 278-300, 306-308, 323, 325, 328-330, 486-489.
Ibid., pp. 248, 266-267, 291-297.
Gupta, R. (1997), Imprints of Four Decades: Scheduled Castes of West Bengal, *Bulletin of the Cultural Research Institute,* Vol. XIX, No. 3, Govt. of West Bengal.
Gupta, R. (1992), Scheduled Castes of West Bengal: A Brief Outline, *Bulletin of the Cultural Research Institute,* Vol. XVIII, No. 3-4, Govt. of West Bengal, p. 1.
Singh, K.S. (2008), *People of India, West Bengal*, Vol. XXXXIII, Anthropological Survey of India, Seagull Books, Calcutta, p. 1056.
Gupta, R. (1992), *op. cit.*, p. 1.
Ghatak, N.K. (1987), Namasudra of Bengal through the Ages, *Bulletin of the Cultural Research Institute*, Vol. XVII, No. 3-4, Govt. of West Bengal, p. 18.
Ibid., p. 18.
Ibid., p. 19.
Risley, H.H. (1998), Tribes and Castes of Bengal, *Ethnographic Glossary*, Firma KLM Private Limited, Calcutta, p. 37.
Singh, K.S. (1995), *The Scheduled Castes*, Oxford University Press, Delhi, p. 64.
Dhali, D.N. and Choudhari, M.K. (1992), Poundra Kshatriya: A Dominant Scheduled Caste Community of West Bengal, *Bulletin of the Cultural Research Institute,* Vol. XVIII, No. 3-4, Govt. of West Bengal, p. 19.
Risley, H.H. (1998), *op. cit.*, p. 71.
Ibid., p. 71.
Ibid., p. 375.
Singh, K.S. (1995), *op. cit.*, p. 443.
Ibid., p. 978.
Biswas, A.K. (2000), *The Namasudra of Bengal*, Blumoon Books, New Delhi, p. 3.
Ghuyre, G.S. (1996), *op. cit.*, p. 52.
Ghatak, N.K. (1987), *op. cit.*
Sarkar, G. (1995), *Jatitattwa Sangraha*, (Bengali) Hiranmoy Sarkar, North 24 Paragana, West Bengal, p. 25.
Sarkar, S. (1382, Bengali Year), *Namasudrai Parsav Bipra*, Khulna Press, Khulna, Bagladesh, p. 81.
Sarkar, G. (1995), *op. cit.*, p. 35.
Biswas, U.N. (2004), *The Strike*, NCMB Memorial Trust, Kolkata, p. 48.
Ibid., p. 48.
Biswas, A.K. (2000), *op. cit.*, pp. 6-7.
Ibid., p. 43.
Ibid., p. 44.
Sarkar, G. (1995), *op. cit.*, p. 46.

III

Scheduled Castes Education in India and Literature

The existence of the present is based on the past. The history of the past provides the structure like which present would be. Too often the review of related literature is seen as a necessary evil to be completed as fast as possible so that one can get on with the study. The review of related literature however is as important as any other component of the research process, and it can be conducted quite possibly if it is approached in an orderly manner. A summary of writings of recognized authorities and of previous research provide evidence that the researcher is familiar with what is already known and what is still unknown and yet to be testified. Besides this, review of related literature helps the researcher to avoid duplication of study and it points out research strategies and specific procedures and measuring instruments that have and have not been found to be productive in investigating problem.

Review of related study assist the researcher academically to proceed in the right direction. According to Van-Dalen's (1973) "The review of educational research gives you an excellent overview of the work that has been done in the fields and helps you keep up with recent development". According to C.V. Good (1959) "Survey of related literature helps us to know whether evidence already available to solve problem adequately without future investigation and thus may save duplication. It may contribute to general scholastic ability if the investigator by providing ideas, theories, theories and explanation, help in formulating the problem and may also suggest the approximate method without research".

Over the last few decades, due to the persistence of differentials between the lower and upper castes, the Scheduled Castes and Scheduled Castes have received special attention in the Governmental policies and in the national level debates and discussions. This has inspired and encouraged researchers to undertake studies on various aspects of Scheduled Castes communities. Studies made by different researchers, scholar, organization and government regarding Scheduled Caste education may be categorize in such way—Studies on Educational Attainment of Scheduled Castes, Studies on Awareness Perception of Scheduled Castes, Studies on Problem faced by Scheduled Castes and Studies related to Wastage, Stagnation and Dropout of Scheduled Castes in various levels of education. In the following discussion, overviews of some of the studies which have investigated and probed into educational conditions of the Scheduled Castes have been examined.

STUDIES ON EDUCATIONAL ATTAINMENT OF SCHEDULED CASTES

Since untouchability was widespread, the first impediment to Scheduled Castes education was discrimination in educational institutions. Therefore, a number of studies undertaken in 1960s and 1970s have investigated the classroom discrimination against Scheduled Caste students. Notable among these are studies by *Jha (1974)*, *Anand (1972)*, *Patwardhan (1973)* and *Sinha (1960)*. Some of the studies have brought out the changing attitude of non-scheduled caste students towards SC students. It is generally true that after independence the attitude of non-scheduled castes towards SC students changed due to legal provisions against untouchability. The studies have also shown that higher caste students have developed favourable attitudes towards the Harijans students.

Benno's (1995), study of certain correlates of academic achievement among Scheduled Castes students in the Urban Territory of Pondicherry examined various correlates of academic achievement including achievement motivation, school adjustment, personality adjustment, gender, birth order, socio-economic status, generation, family type, family size and religion among Scheduled Caste students. The objectives were to study the level of academic achievement, achievement motivation, school adjustment, personality adjustment of Scheduled Castes students in the Union Territory of Pondicherry; to find out the relationship between academic achievement and background variables, i.e. gender, birth order, SES, generation, family type, family size and region; and to identify the predictors of academic achievement among the independent variables. Significant differences were found between Scheduled Caste students grouped on the basis of their adjustment, gender, family type and family size did not differ on their academic achievement.

Gupta, B.S. (1976), conducted a comparative study of educational achievement of scheduled caste and non-scheduled caste students of class X of Uttar Pradesh. The study showed the better performance and achievement by the non-scheduled caste students in comparison to scheduled caste students.

Another study by *Sing, S. (1990)*, shows that in school education the urban scheduled caste students were better in academic achievements. The difference shows the effect of social, family, parental and economic status of them.

A comparative study of the academic achievement of scheduled caste and non-scheduled caste students conducted by *Vyas, U. (1992)* showed that, two groups differ significantly in terms of academic achievement but not in self concept and locus of control.

Venugopal, S., Despande, L.V. and Goyal, J.C. (1992), studied on enrolment and participation of scheduled caste students in secondary level of education. The major findings of the study were the significant difference between the scheduled caste and non-scheduled caste students regarding psychological and economic factors as well as instructional, teaching-learning materials, etc.

The study entitled 'A treatise on the Education of Backward Classes in India since independence with special reference to West Bengal' conducted by *Bandopadhyaya, K.L. (1992)*, showed that, U.E.E. among the backward classes is yet to be achieved. He also found that enrolment of boys in these classes is higher. Absenteeism, wastage and stagnation were found to be higher in case of girls.

An experimental study was performed by *Bibha, R. (1980)*, on 'Self-Concept and other Non-Cognitive factors affecting the academic of the scheduled caste students in Institutions for Higher Technical Education'. The study revealed that (i) The SC students' academic achievement was significantly lower than that of the non-SC students. Both differed significantly with regard to physical self-concept, self-concept, self-esteem and self-concept. (ii) Compared to the non-SC students, the SC students had a low self-concept of academic performance, a high reflected social self concept of mother and peers, and a high reflected self-concept of academic performance of teachers. (iii) There was no difference in the self-concept and reflected self-concept of the SC students except for reflected security, self-concept and self-actualization of teachers. (iv) There was no difference in the SC and the non-SC students with respect of the achievement anxiety and perception of perception of purpose in life.

A study was conducted by *Chitnis, S. (1974)*, on Literacy and Enrolment among the scheduled caste of Maharashtra. The project aimed at finding out (i) whether the investment done by both the centre and the state enabled the scheduled castes to move nearer to the equality promised to them in the constitution, (ii) whether their percentage wise representation in schools and colleges matched their percentage in the population, (iii) whether their distribution between different courses and institutions compared with that of non-scheduled caste population, (iv) whether scheduled caste students enrolled in schools and colleges performed as good as the other students and (v) whether education really equipped the scheduled caste to gain economic and social mobility or whether caste continued to interfere with their advancement. The study revealed that (i) the percentage wise representation of the scheduled caste at schools and colleges in the state as a whole was larger than the percentage of schedule caste in the total population of the state, (ii) the extent of the excess of enrolment over population declined at each successive stage of school and college, (iii) in some district the percentage of scheduled caste enrolment was higher than the percentage of scheduled caste population, but in other districts the reverse was the case; (iv) although the scheduled caste were advanced in the matter of formal education, they lagged behind the total population in literacy; (v) the disparity in literacy between scheduled caste population and the total population was more marked in the urban than in the rural sector, and with respect to males than females.

Duggal, J. (1992), had conducted a study on Access of Scheduled Caste Girls to Elementary Education in Rural Haryana: A study Socio-Economic Problems in Universalisation of Elementary Education: A Micro Study. The objectives of the present study are: (i) Have an understanding of demographic aspect of Scheduled Caste population living in Haryana and district Faridabad including the four sample villages identified in Ballabgarh; (ii) Make a quantitative analysis of existing elementary educational facilities in Haryana in general and district Faridabad in particular with a focus on rural areas; (iii) Make an analysis of educational facilities available to Scheduled Caste girls living in the four sampled villages; (iv) Suggest intervention points to enhance enrolment and retention of the Scheduled Caste girls (6-14) in the identified four villages. The study revealed that increase in the family income had positive effect on the educational status of all the sub-groups of Scheduled Caste girls under study. The study indicated that uniform pattern of giving incentive amount for education of the Scheduled Caste girls irrespective of their economic status was not fair. The incentive amount should vary as per economic conditions of the families of the Scheduled Caste girls. The study indicated that for the achievement of the target of UEE both the parents should be made understand the value of education for their daughter. The elder persons in the Scheduled Caste community can play an important role in bringing this change.

Mishra, Y.N. (1977), had conducted a research on Educational Adaptation, Social Ambition and Performance of Scheduled Caste Students at the Various Educational Levels in the Rewa District of Madhya Pradesh. The following are the salient findings of the study: The Scheduled Caste students had not been able to take full advantage of the facilities and programmes instituted by the government. This was due to certain problems inherent in their social background which continued to hinder their development in the field of education. They also lacked a conducive environment at home which is a pre-requisite for their educational development. The facilities made available to them had not been fully utilized. So far the Scheduled Caste students were concerned; they had generally dropped out at the lower level of their education, and that too due to poverty. Schools had failed in providing development needs of Scheduled Caste students. They did not have any new programme except routine activities which might bring the Scheduled Caste together socially as well as psychologically.

A study was made by *Singh, M. (1980)*, on Social Origins, Educational Attainments and Occupational Mobility among Scheduled Castes in Delhi. The study attempted to answer the following questions: (i) to what extent was son's occupational status associated with that of the father? What was the role of age, marital status, educational attainments and caste and inter-generational occupational mobility? (ii) to what extent did the individual in his job/career move from a lower occupational status to a higher occupational status? (iii) to what extent were the occupational and educational attainments of the Scheduled Castes affected by the number of siblings in the family, by their position among the siblings and by the educational attainments of their father and elder brothers? The major findings were: (i) the majority (59%) of the respondents had fathers who had no schooling and around 30 per cent were educated below high school. (ii) there was a fairly high degree of occupational mobility. (iii) those who moved upwards from manual to white-collar jobs were more likely to be persons with higher educational status and were those who had an elder brother with higher level of education. (iv) there were striking differences between the levels of educational attainments upon entry to the first job and those attained after entering the job. (v) younger sons had higher educational attainments than the eldest son. (vi) father's occupation had the largest influence on son's level of educational attainment.

Singh, P. (1987), had conducted a study on A Comparative Study of Achievement, Adjustment, Attitudes and Problems of First and Subsequent Generation Learners Belonging to Scheduled Castes at Higher Secondary Level. The objectives of the investigation were: (i) to study and compare the enrolment of the first and subsequent generation learners belonging to the Scheduled Caste population; (ii) to study and compare the achievement of the first and subsequent generation learners; (iii) to study and compare the adjustment of the first and subsequent generation learners; (iv) to study and compare the attitudes of the first and subsequent generation learners; (v) to study and compare the problems of the first and subsequent generation learners. The findings were: (i) the enrolment of first generation learners was significantly higher in comparison to the children of subsequent generation learners of the Scheduled Caste community. (ii) Most acute problems of the first generation learners of the Scheduled Castes were: (a) employment during holidays, (b) possibility of post-college education, (c) home being away from the school, (d) lack of facilities at home, (e) desire to be popular.

D'Souza (1980), in his study of the educational level of SCs in Punjab, used 'co-efficient of equality' to indicate the educational attainments of SCs in relation to that of other castes and found enormous differences that persisted between the two.

Aggarwal (1987), while studying the aspects of educational development among the SC population in India, brought out the comparative analysis of literacy situation among the SCs and the general population. The distribution of SCs and the general population was also examined along with various aspects of the identification, measurement and explanation of the socio-economic complexities among SCs. Finally, a vicious type of relationship between levels of educational attainment and other attributes of socio-economic development was also established.

Shashidhar, B. (1981), had conducted a research on a study of the Relationship between a Few School Variables and the Achievement of Scheduled Caste Students Studying in Secondary Schools of Karnataka. The objectives of the investigation were: (i) to study the nature of relationship that existed between organizational climate and the achievement of the Scheduled Caste (SC) students; (ii) to explore the influence of teachers' attitude towards the Scheduled Caste students; (iii) to determine the extent to which the Scheduled Caste students' adjustment in the school influenced their achievement; (iv) to find out the influence of socio-metric status of the Scheduled Caste students on their achievement; (v) to examine the relationship between intelligence and achievement, and to partial out the effect of intelligence on the beverage relationships of other variables with achievement; (vi) to examine the relationship between the students' perception of teachers expectation and the achievement of the Scheduled Caste students. The major findings of the investigation were: (i) openness of the school was significantly related to achievement of the SC students of standards IX and X. (ii) in all the three standards the sociometric status was not significantly related to the achievement of the SC girls, but it was positively and significantly related to the achicvement of the SC boys of standard IX.

The progress of Education of Scheduled castes in Uttar Pradesh had been assessed by *Bindu, R. (1974)*. The major objectives of the study were—(i) to investigate into the progress in literacy and education of the scheduled caste since independence, specially, during the plan period, (ii) to compare the educational development of scheduled castes with that of general population in respect of rate of progress and the areas of gap, (iii) to compare the progress in education in Uttar Pradesh with that of their counterparts in other states, (iv) to study the regional or district wise disparities as well as intra and inter scheduled caste differences in the rate of progress in education, and (v) to examine the effectiveness in implementation of different welfare schemes and their corresponding contribution to educational development of the scheduled castes. The major findings of the study were—(i) Literacy among all the scheduled castes in Uttar Pradesh was lower than in many other states. District wise variation in the percentage of literates was very little. Literacy among scheduled caste females was very low, especially in rural areas. Literacy was highly correlated to urbanization. Sahariya was the most backward caste in literacy. (ii) the enrolment of the scheduled castes at all stages of education showed an increased after independence. (iii) Enrolment growth in primary education during the plan period was higher for the scheduled castes than for other sections of the population. Girls formed only a fifth of this enrolment. Primary education in general had not advanced in the scheduled caste in Uttar Pradesh. (iv) The scheduled castes in a few districts in the western region of the state showed consistently higher rate of growth at every stage of education.

A stratified random sample of the second year students of Bombay University was drawn on the basis of their performance in the university examinations and on the proportion of scheduled caste and non-scheduled caste in the population. Some of the salient findings of the study were: (i) Among the Scheduled Caste students the females were very poorly represented in higher education. (ii) Non-Scheduled Caste students did have a superior educational background. Very few Scheduled Caste students had higher educated parents. (iii) Among the Scheduled Caste and non-Scheduled Caste students, many female students had parents having higher education. (iv) Scheduled Caste students lacked higher occupational and educational background. On the other hand, deficiency of background seemed to be made up by the policies of reservation and other facilities. (v) The Students who came to Bombay from rural areas were much more among the Scheduled Caste students.

Rajpati (1985), investigated the barriers in the primary education of scheduled caste students to finding out if the level of achievement of these pupils differed from that of caste Hindu pupils, as also if the teaching methods factors within these schools, home, environment and health had deleterious effect causing poor academic achievement. The investigation revealed that—1) there was no significant difference in the achievement levels of the pupils in the type of schools studied. All were performing at very low level. 2) Conditions in the schools were far from satisfactory; the teacher pupil ratio was very poor. The teacher had just minimum qualification and had poor training. 3) Method of teaching was found to be defective and not suited to scheduled caste pupils. Teachers were not sincere in discharging their duties. 4) No discriminatory treatment towards scheduled caste pupils as noticed; though not much was done to induce them to achieve better than they were doing. These pupils were made to do work for others. 5) Home background conditions were found to be not encouraging for achievement. The homes had poor facilities, and these were very few persons there who were literate or educated. 6) Most of these pupils suffered from poor eyesight and poor general health.

On the other way, *Gaur, J.S., Thukral, C.M., Jain, V.K., Malik, J.P., Ghosh, Papia, Kaur, Narender* and *Sharma, Sunita* (1988) in their study found that non-scheduled caste high school boys were higher than scheduled caste boys in their self concept as well as intelligence. These differences were more glaring in rural groups.

Again, the study carried out by *Manharlal, Rajyaguru, B. (1992)*, shows that education of scheduled caste children is greatly influenced by the parents education and occupation and socio-familial impact and variables.

Moneyamma, V.G. (1991), in his study revealed that, the comparative enrolment of scheduled caste students in secondary level of education is lower than other community pupil. Moreover, the dropout rate and repeater percentage is higher in case of scheduled caste students than those of non scheduled caste students.

Warudkar, D.S. (1982-86), attempted to identify the barriers in the participation of scheduled caste children in school education. The study revealed that improper physical arrangement, lack of learning materials, books, lack of use of standard regional languages are some major causes of backwardness of scheduled castes in school education.

STUDIES ON AWARENESS PERCEPTION AMONG SCHEDULED CASTES

It is often felt that despite the existence of a variety of facilities and incentives for SC and ST students, the awareness level of these facilities among the students and their parents is low. Therefore, a good number of research studies have been conducted during 1970s, 1980s and 1990s to examine these questions. Some studies have found a difference in the awareness of parents belonging to scheduled castes about importance of education and educational schemes for scheduled castes.

Premi, (1974), Punalekar, (1975), et al. found that the parents were aware of the educational concessions, scholarships, stipends, reservation of seats for admission to educational institutions provided by Govt./ Harijan Welfare Department. However the researcher like—*Naik (1971), Maurya (1976), Yadav (1979), Nautiyal (1986), et al.* had found that the respondents were still unaware about the various facilities, aids, concessions and other programmes provided by the government for the welfare of the scheduled caste. Taken together, the studies have presented a mixed bag of findings in this area.

An investigation was conducted by *Yadav, S.K. (1981)*, on 'Study of the Scheduled Castes' Awareness about the schemes for their Educational Progress. The objectives of the investigation were: (i) to identify the educational schemes for facilitating education of the children belonging to SCs; (ii) to study the awareness of students and the heads of families regarding the educational schemes for the facilitating education of the children belonging to SCs (iii) to study the sources of awareness about the educational schemes for the facilitating education of the children belonging to SCs; (iv) to study the antecedent variables of the awareness level of heads of families regarding the educational schemes for the facilitating education of the children belonging to SCs; (v) to study the relationship between the awareness of heads of about the educational schemes and their utilization by the children belonging to SCs. The findings of the study were: (i) The school was the major sources of awareness for parents about the educational schemes. (ii) The students in the urban areas had a higher awareness than those in the semi-urban and rural areas. (iii) The awareness level of the male students was higher than that of the female students in the total sample. (iv) Association was found between the castes within the Scheduled Castes and the awareness level of the heads of the families irrespective of location areas to which they belonged. (v) The congruence between the awareness of the heads of the families and the students was further corroborated by the significant correlations. (vi) The annual income of the heads of the families as well as the per capita income differed in different location areas, namely, rural, urban and semi-urban. (vii) Association was found between the awareness of heads of the families and the utilization of the educational schemes by their wards. (viii) The educational level of the head of the family varied from area to area. The awareness of the heads of the families was associated with their educational level except in rural areas.

Jain, Vidyut (1988), studied the interests and values of school students belonging to Scheduled Castes and backward classes. The study found the differences between the rural and urban community regarding the interests and values of the Scheduled Castes students and backward students.

Abbasyulu (1977), and *Yadav (1983)*, found that scheduled caste elite group was more conscious about the education and various schemes for scheduled caste students provided by the government. Consequently their progress is a lot higher than the lower group of scheduled caste.

Singh, G. (1988), had researched on Teacher's Perception of Scheduled Caste Students and Their Scholastic Achievement. The study was taken the following objectives in view: (i) to find out the teachers' perception of Scheduled Caste students, viz., A-non Scheduled Caste teachers perception of Scheduled Caste students, B-Scheduled Caste teachers perception of Scheduled Caste students; (ii) to find out the distance between non-Scheduled Caste teachers and Scheduled Caste students, between non-Scheduled Caste teachers and non-Scheduled Caste students and between the two categories of the students in semantic space of non-Scheduled Caste teachers; (iii) to find out the distance between Scheduled Caste teacher and Scheduled Caste students, between Scheduled Caste teachers and non-Scheduled Caste students and between both categories of students in semantic space of Scheduled Caste teachers;

(iv) to find out the relationship between teachers perception of Scheduled Caste students and their scholastic achievement. The major conclusions drawn from the findings of the present study are: (i) There is a caste bias in the perception of Scheduled Caste and non-Scheduled Caste teachers both. (ii) It is further concluded that the non-Scheduled Caste teachers are likely to discriminate between Scheduled Caste students and non-Scheduled students more prominently than Scheduled Caste teachers (perceiver) do with non-Scheduled Caste students and Scheduled caste students (perceived). (iii) The Scheduled Caste students perceive their teacher closer to themselves than do the non-Scheduled Caste students. (iv) Both categories of students and teachers have positive self perception on all the perceptional dimensions. (v) The non-scheduled Caste teachers maintain larger distance between the Scheduled Caste and non-Scheduled Caste students than do the Scheduled Caste teachers. (vi) It is further concluded that the non-Scheduled Caste teachers perception of Scheduled Caste students in directly related to their scholastic achievement. But Scheduled Caste teachers' perception of Scheduled Caste student is inversely related to their scholastic achievement.

A study was carried out by *Pandey, P.N. (1979)*, on education and social mobility among scheduled caste with the following objectives—i) to examine critically the functional role of education in bring about social mobility ii) to analyze the nature, trend and emerging patterns of social mobility iii) to explain how far they were changing their social images by adopting higher Hindu caste manners etc. iv) to find whether the concept of sanskritazisation was applicable in this context and v) to trace a functional alternative for sanskritazisation and westernization. The major findings of the research were—1) The growth of modern education and the changing socio economic status among the scheduled caste were closely related to each other. 2) Among the educated there was strong reluctance to traditional social status and occupational structure. 3) Education positive discrimination and democratic secularism were very helpful. They were more achievement oriented than astrictive oriented. 4) Not getting sanskritized in the rituals, practices, etc. Of the higher castes they aspired to imitate the elite sections of any caste, class or culture in urbanized and westernized values. 5) The emergence of high men of the scheduled caste in government job of prestige and power was another adaptive change. 6) The highly educated and those who had an educated social standing formed and exclusive group to move upward by seeking marital relations among the upper castes and from contacts with the elite section of the society. They did recognize their obligations towards their caste fellowman that had a low social and economic status. 7) Elite emulation was the basis for structural mobility rather than cultural and ritual mobility through sanskritisation.

A study entitled "Identity of scheduled caste students" carried out by Chitnis, S. (1981), keeping ahead the following objectives-i) to study the identity of the scheduled caste verses the caste Hindu school students ii) to study the relationship between the socio economic status and the identity of the students iii) to compare the identity of the scheduled caste students studying in school managed by different organization iv) to study sex differences in the identity of the scheduled caste students and v) to study the relationship between the level of education and the identity among the scheduled caste students.

D'soura (1980), studied educational inequalities among scheduled caste. The major objective of the study was to unfold the structural differentiation of the educational equalities among the scheduled caste. The investigator attempted to find out the response for i) the slow rate of narrowing the educational gap between the scheduled caste and rest of the society ii) the inequalities among the scheduled caste themselves and iii) the widening educational gaps among the scheduled caste. The major finding of the study were—1) It was assumed that the educational inequalities between the scheduled caste and rest of the society were due to the long standing socio economic exploitation of the former by the rest of the society. 2) Remedial measure by way of protective discrimination taken by the state had succeeded, although to a minute extent as was clear from 1971 educational data report in so far as the educational inequality between the scheduled caste and the rest of the society was concerned but among the scheduled caste themselves they were acting with greater vigour.

Vaishnav (1983), investigated the educational and occupational experiences of the scheduled caste post matric scholars of Ahmedabad City. This was a follow up study in 1977 of a sample of scheduled caste post matric scholars residing in Ahmedabad city who had been studied earlier in 1967-68. The major objectives of the study were to analyze the educational and occupational experiences of the sample. It was also tried to find out the outcomes of their educational and occupational experiences such as attitudes towards education of their own children. A sample of 226 (181 males and 45 females) SC post Matric scholars for examining different aspects (educational and occupational attainment, reasons for dropping out and failures, motivations for further study, experiences with the non SC, difficulties encountered during and after post Matric study were selected.

Chitnis (1981), conducted a study entitled on "A long way to go—Report on a survey of scheduled caste High school and college students in 15 states of India. The objectives of the study were to find out how the various types of facilities provided for promoting education among the scheduled caste and the ST children had been made use of and what kinds of problems were faced by these children in the process of education. The study was conducted in two phases. The first phase consisted of preparing a statistical profile of the scheduled caste and scheduled tribe population indicating demographic characteristics of the scheduled caste and scheduled tribes in the state, describing facilities available to them and indicating government and voluntary agencies working for their advancement. The second phase consisted of a field study on several aspects of the students (high school and college) level. The major findings were—1. The respondent scheduled caste students were unable to escape their low caste identity and their classmate's behaviour towards them was affected by this knowledge. 2. They belonged to poor uneducated family, but at the same time were highly selected elite who had been able to overcome the shortcomings in their backgrounds and were able to progress without failure to high school and college. 3. They showed an ability to overcome the handicap on ability to overcome the handicap of the home background and had encouraging parents 4. There were inter sex, inter caste and interstate disparities in terms of educational advancement of scheduled caste.

Sabnis Mahurkar (1985), studied the relationship between education and social status of scheduled caste students from Breed district. The main objectives of the study were to study whether or not the social status of scheduled caste men and woman had improved as a result of graduation. The sample comprised all scheduled caste students who graduated in 1967, 1972, 1977 from all the colleges of Breed district. They observed that the economic condition of graduates had improved as a result of education and had improved the life style and social status of scheduled caste students.

Kulkarni (1985), examined the availability of facilities such as text books, library, accommodation, food, and medical help etc. to scheduled caste students. The major objectives were—(i) to study the extent to which education and other facilities were available to scheduled caste students of Jalana District and (ii) to make recommendation to improve facilities available to them. A printed questionnaire was used for the purpose of data collection. The study revealed that facilities required for study among the scheduled caste students were not sufficient so far as their home, economic condition and other facilities are concerned.

Gogate, S.B. (1985), examined the availability of scholarships and other financial facilities to scheduled caste students in Maharastra. Four rural schools and four urban schools were selected for study. An attempt also made to choose institutions having hostel facilities or institutions at plus where there were government hostels. The information was collected through questionnaire. The result suggested that in the absence of scholarship scheme in the school children from rural areas and poor families could not join even the primary school and remained illiterate. Again it showed that in spite of govt. scholarships and hostel accommodation many students were not able to show progress in studies, probably because of their poor economic condition at their home and lack of facilities in the hostels.

Pal, R.A. (1984), studied the personality patterns of scheduled caste in comparison to high caste students. As a sample 200 scheduled caste students and 200 high caste students were selected from 60 Govt. high school of Haryana. The students were administered the cattle high school personality questionnaire—The Allport-Vernon and Lindzey Inventory of values. The Deo personality world list, Raven's standard progressive Matrics and the Rao socio-economic status Rating scale. The result showed that scheduled caste students were more reserved, expedient, shy, tough minded, tense and had in disciplined self conflict. On the other hand, high caste students were more outgoing, conscientious, venturesome, tender minded, controlled and relaxed.

A study of Locus Control and general Intelligence among scheduled caste and non-scheduled caste students was conducted by *Aggarwal, Y.P. (1975)*. The objectives of the study were—(i) to find out the differences in personality on the dimension of locus of control among students of scheduled castes and non-scheduled castes; and (ii) to find out the differences in general intelligence among the two groups. The following were the main conclusion of the study—1) significant differences in the mean locus control scores existed between the two groups. 2) The scheduled castes group was found to be more external (believing in systems luck and chance for its accomplishments) than the non-scheduled caste group. 3) Significant differences existed between the two groups in the mean intelligence scores, the non-scheduled castes group being significantly more intelligent, on the average, than the scheduled caste group.

Aggarwal, Y. and et al. (1992), studied about the educating scheduled castes; to find out firstly, the historical process of identification of scheduled castes in India to highlight the changes that have taken place in their identification criterion since independence; secondly, to analyze the patterns of spatial concentration/dispersion of SCs in different parts of the country; thirdly, to examine whether SCs can be considered as internally homogeneous group as far as their caste composition, educational and socio-economic development is concerned, fourthly, to identify the spatial patterns of literacy for SCs as whole and in relation to NSS highlighting rural-urban male-female, SC-NS and inter-district differentials wherever possible, fifth, identification of the spatial patterns of educational development among the SC population and more specifically among the literate SCs, sixth, to critically examine various measures of disparities particularly those related to the measurement of differentials between 'haves' and 'have-nots' and to suggest the appropriate measures to be used in the study, seventh, to examine the work participation rate among various strata of SC population and to relate it to their educational attainment etc. In this study comprehensive set of data pertaining to the number of educated and literate persons and some associated aspects of socio-economic development are collected every ten years on a census basis in India. An important outcome of the study is the assertion that not all SCs are backward and not non-scheduled castes are better-off. The complexities of spatial dispersion, economies of agglomeration and the occupational stratification intertwine to produce complex patterns, where the distinction between SCs and non SC population gets blurred at many times. There are certain scheduled castes whose socio-economic base can be compared to that of the best among the Non-scheduled and there are caste groups who are the most backward. Keeping these factors in view, the study has identified various topologies having bearing on the programmes of educational development.

Economic status also increases the awareness of scheduled castes about educational opportunities, educational schemes and enrolment and continuation of study. The rise in income of the family increases the awareness as well as enrolment of children in schools *(Shanthakumari, 1976, Yadav, 1983 and Yadav, 1987).*

Aggarwal, Archana (1992), in her Doctoral research entitled 'social, psychological and educational study of the scheduled castes students studying in high school of Lucknow city' studied the socio economic status, academic achievement, intelligence, self concept and occupational aspirations of scheduled castes students. The study found that, scheduled castes students to be inferior to non-scheduled castes students in terms of socio economic status, self concept, occupational aspirations and academic achievement but the scheduled caste students did not differ from the non-scheduled caste students in terms of their intelligence. Scheduled caste girls were found to be higher than their male counterparts. Only the occupational aspiration of scheduled caste girls was lower than that of their male counterparts.

The study by *Bej, Jayprakash (1991),* entitled 'A descriptive study of the general intelligence and creativity of scheduled caste students' of class v-viii showed that scheduled caste students' were parallely intelligent and creative to their non-scheduled caste counterparts.

The study conducted by *Mishra, S.C. (1991),* examined the relationship between the education and the social status of scheduled caste students at secondary level of education of Cuttack District in Orissa. The study showed that, education has a considerable impact on their economic conditions but due to limited aspirations, job insecurity and poverty the majority of scheduled caste respondents are not encouraged to opt for secondary or higher education.

A study of the 'Effect of facilities given by the government to the backward class pupils in secondary schools in Devgad Taluka of Maharastra' was carried by *Kamble, P.R. (1992),* found that the facilities provided to the students of the backward classes improved their attendance and pass percentage and reduced dropout rate.

Besides, *Aggarwal (1976), Pankaj (1978)*, and Lakshmanna (1984) reported that corrupt practices and misappropriation of funds and lack of supervision by the government authorities affects scheduled caste enrolment and retention in both school and college level of education. In this regard *Rajagopalan (1974), Singh (1979), Desai (1979)* and *Azad (1983)* found that general economic position of scheduled castes is so poor that in spite of scholarships they are unable to pursue education. Premi (1974, 1984), found that at elementary school stage it could be possible to study without financial support but she found it is difficult to continue education at secondary stage and in higher education without financial support. Financial concessions are important motivating force for the respondents. The corrupt practices in administration and misappropriation of funds are accompanied by the inadequacy of educational facilities. Most of the students and parents belonging to scheduled caste category report that the existing amount of schemes and scholarships are grossly inadequate and even they found it difficult to meet the cost of notebooks *(Goyal, 1974, Rajagopalan, 1976, Parvathamma, 1977, Rath, 1981, Dasai, 1975, Singh, 1987, Sharma, 1983, Trivedi, 1987, and Yadav 1983).*

An independent study taken up by *Srivastava, L.R.N. (1988-90)*, was 'An evaluative study of the pre-matric scholarships scheme meant for Scheduled Castes. The results showed interstate variation. The common finding was that not only was the amount of scholarships inadequate, it was not even disbursed in time. It was also found that money received by the students was spent for purposes other than educational.

Sachinadananda and Sinha, Ramesh, P. (1989), conducted a study of Scheduled Castes with a view to find out how the educational facilities have been used by the target groups and what types of problems are faced by them in the process of education. The study suggested reframing of the strategy for the education of the Scheduled Castes, diverting 50 per cent of the scholarship amount for strengthening school education, making appointment of teachers from the same community in case school population has more S.C. students, ensuring availability of facilities to most disadvantaged one.

Dubey, S.M. (1974), had researched on Study of Scheduled Caste and Scheduled Tribe Students in Assam. The main objectives of the study are: (i) to identify difference in backwardness between the difference castes and tribes; (ii) to provide some insights into the functioning of selected institutions and organizations; (iii) to probe into the problems of Scheduled Caste and Scheduled Tribes teachers; (iv) job opportunities; and (v) hostel facilities etc. Some of its findings are: (i) Irrespective of their financial position, majority of respondents aspire to obtain post-graduate degrees. (ii) As regards occupational aspirations, 69.9 per cent Scheduled Caste and 54.5 per cent Scheduled Tribe students have given first preference to self-employment. (iii) Largest number of respondents feel that the administration of the government programmes for the welfare of Scheduled Castes and Scheduled Tribes is fairly satisfactory. Majority of students expressed satisfaction on the policy of reservation of seats in education institutions and government jobs. (iv) There is undue delay in disbursement of scholarship money.

The study was made by *Dubey, S.N. (1982)*, on Reaction to Frustration as a function of Personality Factors and Need Patterns of Scheduled Caste Adolescents and Young Adults. The objectives of the study were: (i) to examine the ways in which adolescents and young adults of the Scheduled Caste reacted in a frustrating situation, (ii) to find out differences in the pattern of hierarchy of reaction to frustration between the two age groups, (iii) to explore the personality and need correlates and differentials of extreme reactions to frustrations, and (iv) to examine the factorial structure of reactions to frustration in relation to personality and need variables among the Scheduled Caste subjects. The findings of the study were: (i) the Scheduled Caste (SC) adolescents had significantly higher means on ego-defensive and extra aggressive and regressive reactions as compared to the non-SC ones. (ii) Reserveness, sobriety, expediency, carefulness, conservatism, group dependence, tense and tender-mindedness were found to be the personality characteristics of the OD responses. (iii) Non-SC adolescents' OD responses were characterized by reserveness (factor A), threat sensitivity (factor H) and low integration (factor Q3).

Gogate, S.B. (1985), had conducted a study on A Critical Study of the Scholarships and Other Financial Facilities to Scheduled Caste Students in Marathwada. The major objectives were:(i) to ascertain the facts in relation to the availability of scholarships and other financial facilities to Scheduled caste (SC) students in Marathwada, and (ii) to suggest improvements in the procedure of granting and distributing scholarships to SC students. Some of the conclusions were: (i) all the principals and students demanded that the rate of scholarships be linked with the cost of living index. (ii) Most parents of SC students were landless labourers. They had large families to maintain. This showed that children from these families could take education only with the help of government scholarships. (iii) most of the students complained about the non-availability of facilities in SC hostels. The food was invariably bad and students suspected corruption in hostel administration. It was necessary that an inspection panel regularly visited these hostels. Similarly there should be no distinction in regard to payment of grants to government and non-government BC hostels.

Jain, N.P. (1984), had conducted a study on Culture Stratum and Personality Factors as Correlates of Parenting (Fathering) in High, Backward and Scheduled Caste People of Mainpuri District (Uttar Pradesh). The objectives of the study were: (i) to study parenting with a view to determining a typical characteristics of parents as related to personality factors, culture stratum and caste, (ii) to explore the mutually affecting roles, as well as the directions among personality factors, culture stratum and caste while contributing to parenting to parenting with simultaneous operations, (iii) to evolve an operational structure for parenting in terms of various defined roles so that its expanding connotations may provide a useful aid to future research in the area, (iv) to explore new vistas with additional insights in the vitally important field to parenting through a multivariate study programme, and (v) to explore new problem areas in the field that demand appropriate and useful researches and are promising in terms of their future prospects. The findings were: (i) fathering of hate towards children was a rural phenomenon. It related to people of the Scheduled Castes. (ii) Fathering of love towards children characteristically related to urban high caste and to rural Scheduled Caste parents. (iii) Fathering of democratic behaviour towards children was a function of emotional dryness. It was a characteristic of Scheduled Caste parenting. It was urban in strong ego and rural in weak ego parents. (iv) Fathering of autocratic treatment of children was a low caste phenomenon and was characteristically a byproduct of high ego tension. (v) Fathering of independency towards children was characteristically affectothymic. (vi) Fathering of dependency towards children was a low-caste phenomenon and belonged to related rural parents.

Kakkar, S.P. (1990), had conducted a researched on The Personality Characteristics and Educational Problems of Scheduled Caste Students. Specific objectives of the study are: (i) to determine whether the personality differences, if any are attributable to educational problems, or socio-economic status or both, (ii) to determine the differences between SC and other students in personality and educational problems, (iii) to determine whether personality or socio-economic status effects educational problems in the case of each population group, (iv) to determine whether personality differences, or differences in educational problems are attributable to Scheduled Caste factor. The findings were: Scheduled Caste students have all the personality characteristics that are a prerequisite to progress in life. They are higher than others in vigor and ascendancy. They are high on educational problems and low in socio-economic level. Scheduled Caste students need specific personality oriented programmes in pre-school and early childhood education.

A study entitled 'Survey of the Provision, Administration and Effective Utilization of Facilities such as Textbooks, Libraries , Living Accommodation, Meals, Health Services Available to Students of Scheduled Castes in Aurangabad District' by Kaldate, S. (1974), keeping ahead the following objectives—(i) to examine the extent to which educational and other facilities were available to Scheduled Caste students of Aurangabad district, and (iii) to make recommendations to improve facilities available to Scheduled caste students.

Nagaraju, C.S. (1977), was conducted a researched on A study of a few Social Factors Affecting Scholastic Achievement of Scheduled Caste Students Studying in Secondary Schools of Karnataka. The objectives of the study were: (i) to get a descriptive picture of the Scheduled Caste Students separately, in three standards, in terms of their socio-psychological characteristics and demographic features, (ii) to find out the level of their educational achievement as compared to the population in general, and (iii) to relate the socio-psychological and demographic characteristics with their educational achievement. The following were the major findings: (i) as a group, the Scheduled Caste students came from lowest socio-economic strata. They had a moderate positive self-concept. (ii) self-concept was found to be significantly related with achievement. (iii) Occupational aspirations were found to be significantly related with achievement. (iv) the aspirational inputs and the socio-economic status of the family were found to be related with achievement only in the case of the standard X students. (v) educational aspirations were found to be related with achievement in standard VIII and IX. (vi) sociometric status was found to be related with achievement at the standard IX level.

Navare, S.R. (1990), had researched on The Role of Education in Socialization of Scheduled Caste Women: A Case study of Primary School Teachers in Pune. Following were the objectives of the study: (i) to study the influence of education and the socialization of women which enables her to improve her status within the family and within the society; (ii) to study the influence of teaching profession on the socialization of SC women and the study to extend to which it improves their status and enriches their personality; (iii) to study the influence of castes in the specialization of SC women and to study to extend to which caste has affected their status and role in the family. (iv) to study whether rural and urban origin influences socialization of SC women teachers differently. Regarding the hypotheses in relation to the influence of education, it was found that education plays an important role in developing social behaviour and attitude towards others. When a Scheduled Caste women teacher were compared with illiterate women the real effect of education was very evident. The effect of caste and profession on socialization of Scheduled Caste women teacher in her personal interviews with the respondent their feeling of importance of education, attitude towards family, status of the family and identity as women was evident in their interviews.

Prakash, O. (1981), had researched on A study of some Psycho-Social Variables among Caste Hindu and Scheduled Caste Children in the Rural Set-Up. The objective of the study was to investigate five Psycho-Social Variables among Caste Hindu and Scheduled Caste Children in the Rural Set-Up. The variables studied were the intellectual level of the groups, the socio-economic status of parents. their concept of self, social prejudice as practiced and aggression, frustration, etc. The findings indicated: (i) the caste Hindu children had a significantly better self-concept. (ii) The caste Hindu children scored significantly higher than Scheduled Caste Children on the social prejudice scale; they scored higher on two sub-scales, class differences and caste system. (iii) Significant differences existed between the caste Hindu and Scheduled Caste children on ego-defensive and need persistence types of reactions, the former scoring higher on the ego-defensive and the latter on the need-persistence. There was no difference as regards obstacle-dominance type of reactions. (iv) When compared on super ego factor dimension, the Scheduled Caste children scored higher than caste Hindu children. (v) Factor analysis for the P.F. study data indicated seven factors, namely, assertive and self-critical domination attitude, low integration, negativism and apprehensiveness, preference for one's own decisions, obtrusiveness and aggressiveness, escapist attitude, and self-opinion for the caste Hindu group.

Prajapati, G.K. (1982), was conducted a study on Impact of Education on Social, Economic and Political Changes Among Scheduled Castes: A Case Study of Danapore Sub-Division. The study aimed at assessing the social consequences of education among the Scheduled Castes. The main findings of the study was that education had not been able to loosen the caste ties and they (Scheduled Castes) were in favour of continuance of the caste system. The main reason for such a feeling among the SC was the advantage they were getting from the reservation policy.

A study conducted by *Premala, B.D. (1986)*, on A study of the Extent and Problems of Educational Facilities Offered by the Government of Karnataka to the SCs at the Primary School Stage with Special Reference to Bangalore District. The objective of the study were: (i) to examine the growth and pattern of enrolment of Scheduled Castes (SC); (ii) to examine the utilization of special educational facilities offered to Scheduled Castes by the Karnataka Government since 1961 during the third five year plan; (iii) to compare the growth and enrolment of Scheduled Castes and non-Scheduled Castes; (iv) to study in depth the problems faced by SC children in enrolment and utilization of facilities; (v) to make an in depth case study of selected beneficiaries. The findings indicated: (i) late enrolment of children need for children to work at home non-availability of higher primary schools within walking distance and lack of commuting facilities were identified as some of the major problems of enrolment and non utilization of educational facilities. (ii) historical factors in the form of better educational atmosphere, traditions and records of performance, in addition to non-historical factors such as organizational and administrative efforts were identified as promoting enrolment growth as well as growth rate.

A research conducted by *Premi, K.K. (1977)*, on Protective Legislation and Equality of Educational Opportunity: A Study of Scheduled Castes in Punjab. The objective of the study were: (i) to measure the extent of equality for the Scheduled Castes vis-à-vis non-Scheduled Castes in respect to equality within educational system and to study the trend with regard to it over the last two decades, from 1950-1951 to 1970-71; (ii) to estimate the extent of equality for the Scheduled Castes vis-a vis others in terms of post-school performance; (iii) to assess the role of protective privileges in the educational advancement of the Scheduled Castes as perceived by them and explain the emerging inequalities in the context of privileges. The findings of the study pointed out that equality of educational opportunity for Scheduled Castes as compared to the non-Scheduled Castes was still a distant goal, even in terms of equal access to educational institutions. The aspects of equality in terms of equal inputs had not so far been accepted in principle. Education, to a certain extent, at higher levels, had been able to bridge the gap in the earnings of the two groups, but was incapable of erasing the influence of social origin. A distinct caste and class pattern in the use of educational facilities at the higher stage was observed.

Devi, R. (1990), had conducted a researched on A Note on the Education of Scheduled Caste Population in Urban Trivandrum. In the present paper it is proposed to examine the educational situation of the Scheduled Caste population in general and that of the numerically important Scheduled Caste population in particular in urban Trivandrum for the years 1961-1971 and1981. An examination of the census information pertaining to the education of the Scheduled Caste population in urban Trivandrum shows that the level is lower than that of the non-Scheduled Castes but the gap is setting bridged fast over the years. Thus the social upliftment of the Scheduled Caste population seems to be rather fast in this urban area, gauging from their educational development.

Singh, R.P. (1982), had researched on Educational Backwardness of Scheduled Caste Students and a Need-Oriented Plan for Their Development. The objectives of the investigation were: (i) assessment of educational backwardness of the Scheduled Castes in terms of their enrolment ratio at the various levels of education as compared to the general population, their development rate at various educational levels and their performance at various educational levels as compared to the general educational standard, (ii) identification of their social, economic, educational and political needs, (iii) preparation of a plan for their educational development so as to satisfy their needs. The findings were: (i) at the lower level of education, 41.5 per cent had nuclear families as compared to 10.2 per cent at the higher levels. (ii) four percent guardians of the higher level students and teachers were illiterate implying speedy educational transmission from generation to generation.

A study entitled 'The education of the Scheduled Castes and Their Development Needs since Independence (1947) in the Varanasi Educational Region' was made by *Singh, S.D. (1981)*. The objectives of the investigation were: (i) to determine the quantitative and the qualitative growth of education of the Scheduled Caste population since Independence, (ii) to determine the existing position of the education of the scheduled Castes; (iii) to make an extensive survey of the existing educational facilities (along with institutions) for the Scheduled Castes at different levels, (iv) to suggest educational measures for the development of the scheduled Caste population in this region. The major Findings were: (i) Teachers, as a class, did not discriminate between the Harijan students. (ii) College teachers were mostly engaged in political affairs. It brought disturbance in teaching. (iii) Schools had turned into political area instead of being temples of learning and knowledge. (iv) The Harijan students failed to manage private tuitions due to economic distress.

Singh, S.N. (1972), had researched on A Study of the Pattern of Educational and Occupation of Persons Living in Varanasi (Rural) with Special Reference to Scheduled Castes. The present study aimed at investigating the pattern of occupation and education in the rural areas of Varanasi in various socio-economic groups, whether there had been any change in this pattern over time and if so. whether the change was inform in different groups. It also tried to see how far the goal of universal primary education had been achieved and thereby tried to pinpoint the factors which caused 'dropout' of the children below fifteen years of age. The study revealed the following facts: (i) The distribution of workers in various occupations differed from caste to caste. (ii) The percentage of workers engaged in agriculture decreased with increase in education. (iii) The percentage of workers in government service increased with education. (iv) There was a gradual shift in occupation over time from agriculture to non-agriculture. A shift was also observed among the occupation over time also depended on caste and education.

Tribhuvan, U.D. (1977), had conducted a researched on A study of Educated Scheduled Caste Women in an Urban Setting. The objectives of the investigation were: (i) to understand the role of education in bringing about the desired changes to help the educated Scheduled Caste women in their upward movement, and (ii) to know the acceptance of the educated Scheduled Caste women by the wider society on the basis of equality of opportunity. The findings were: (i) due to higher education, the Scheduled Caste women achieved a high status, which was unknown in their family and community. The respondents reported that education was helpful in reducing the caste barriers and therefore the Scheduled Caste women could easily adjust themselves to higher-class people. (ii) the education of Scheduled Caste women had resulted in bringing about profound changes in their attitude towards marriage.

An investigation was conducted by *Waghmare, J.M. (1985)*, on A Study of Relationship between Education and Social Status among Scheduled Caste Students. The objective of the investigation was to find out whether Scheduled Caste (SC) graduates had risen up in social status due to graduation. The results obtained were: (i) one hundred and fifty members of families of these graduates were engaged in occupations requiring no specific skills. They were engaged in sundry jobs. (ii) all the students were graduates. (iii) forty-four had a monthly income of more than Rs. 1000.56 had monthly income of less than Rs. 1000, out of whom 22 earned less than Rs. 200 per month. (iv) seventy-three persons had been staying in houses constructed of bricks and mud. Moreover they had to stay in localities of their own castes. (v) six families had part-time of full-time servants. (vi) generally, these families had middle class neighbors. (vii) most of the families had no local means of survival. They had to allow their children to migrate to other places for education and jobs.

An investigation was conducted by *Yadav, S.K. (1985)*, on Educational Schemes for Scheduled Caste Teachers' Perception Profile. The objectives of the investigation were: (i) to identify the educational schemes aiming at facilitating education of the children belonging to SCs; (ii) to study the perception of the teachers regarding the educational schemes directed at facilitating the education of the children belonging to SCs identified at (1) above; (iii) to study the teacher's perception of the problems which they face in utilizing the education of their children; (iv) to study the directions for procedural modifications with a view to facilitating utilization of the educational schemes by the SCs with particular reference to the conditions of eligibility value of scholarships selection of candidates, duration and renewal of awards, mode of payment mode of publicity and submitting applications; (v) to study the problems of those students belonging to the Scheduled Caste who do not avail of the educational facilities despite being eligible for them; (vi) to the causes and remedies of the dropout students belonging to SCs; (vii) to study the teachers perception of the academic achievement of the Scheduled Castes. The findings of the study were: (i) educational schemes provided by government are inadequate and unsatisfactory, the way the considerable number of teachers visualized it. (ii) students go far part work to finance themselves to pursue their education. (iii) Inadequate information on educational schemes. (iv) Indifferent attitude of the officials towards these sections. (v) Income level is very low. (vi) The requirement of formalities to fill-up the form is lengthy process and should be abolished. (vii) the mode of payment has to be made in installment basis so that they can utilize it in proper manner.

STUDIES RELATED TO THE PROBLEMS OF SCHEDULED CASTE STUDENTS

A number of studies have examined the questions related to the problems faced by the SC students at various levels of education. in fact there are many institution related factors which influence the retention and achievement levels of SC students and are the root cause of high disparities in educational attainment between SC population and general population and within the various castes comprising SCs.

A study was made by Upadhyay, *H.C. (1981)*, on The Problems of Scheduled Castes in the Kumaun Hills: A Sociological Study. The objectives of the investigation were: (i) to explore the prevailing conditions of the untouchables in Kumaun region and to expose those social situations which caused the autocratic behaviour of the upper-caste people, (ii) to trace out the factors and causes of backwardness among the untouchable castes, (iii) to evaluate the impact of government welfare measures , (iv) to unearth the socio-cultural milieu in order to reconstruct the inter-caste relationships patterns, (v) to suggest guidelines for social planning and policy formation for the upliftment of the untouchables in the Kumaun hills. The results obtained were: (i) most of the Harijan families (74%) were nuclear in nature. (ii) illiteracy among the Harijan males was less (52.08%) than that among the females (82,58%). (iii) the literate persons showed a more favourable attitude towards their parents. (iv) the untouchable population in general was found to be underpaid and belonged to the low-earning group. (v) the main causes found responsible for socio-economic backwardness were social deprivation, economic exploitation and lack of opportunity.

Puran S. (1989), had researched on Problems of Education Among Scheduled Caste: A Comparative Study of Achievement, Adjustment, Attitudes and Problems of First and Subsequent Generation Learners Belonging to Scheduled Caste at Higher Education. The study has been designed to achieve the following objectives: (i) to study and compare the enrolment of the first and subsequent generation learners belonging to the Scheduled Caste population; (ii) to study and compare the achievement of the first and subsequent generation learners; (iii) to study and compare the adjustment of the first and subsequent generation learners; (iv) to study and compare the attitude of the first and subsequent generation learners; (v) to study and compare the attitudes of the first and subsequent generation learners towards society. The findings indicated: (i) enrolment in class XI was found higher in case of the first and subsequent generation learners as compared to that of the subsequent generation learners of the Scheduled Castes. (ii) so far as achievement is concerned no significance difference was found between the first and subsequent generation learners of Scheduled Caste. (iii) the attitudes such as towards colleges, education and society do not make any significant difference between the first and second generation.

A study entitled, "Educational Problems of Scheduled Caste Students in the Punjab: School Students" was made by Pimpley, *P.N. (1974)*, the study aimed at surveying the socio-economic background of the Scheduled Caste (SC) students from the Punjab. The author tried to assess the status of the SC students their performance at school, their feeling of social distance, their opinion about the facilities for them, and thereby tried to show how these could be problematic in their educational aspirations. The findings indicated: (i) SC school students were mainly male, unmarried and belonged to four major castes namely, Addharmi, Balmiki, Majhabi and Ramdasia. (ii) parents were almost illiterate, economic condition of the family was 'difficult' and the father's occupation was mainly farming. (iii) SC students mainly spent a fair amount of time for studies, they could follow the class, their educational aspirations were very high and they aspired for while collar jobs, yet their dropout rate were quite high. (v) They were inferior in their academic caliber as opined by their teachers. (vi) Government servants and national leaders were most popular to SC students. (vii) They were not much exposed to mass media and, therefore, politicization was low.

A study entitled, "Educational Problems of Scheduled Caste Students in the Punjab: College Students" was made by Pimpley, *P.N. (1974)*, the study was undertaken to investigate the educational problems of the Scheduled Caste (SC) college students of Punjab. The author tried to see how their education affected their social outlook, their attitude towards government assistance and finally their opinion about the status of SC, in general. The findings indicated: (i) SC school college students were mostly over-aged; male students were over represented in the sample; about ninety percent of them were unmarried and mainly Hindus rather than Sikhs. (ii) Most of them could follow the class and wastage was not very high. (iii) Their educational as well as occupational aspirations were very high. (iv) They had no experience of ill treatment. (v) Most of them considered endogamy and parental authority as most important. (vi) they also felt that the status of SC had improved, but was still inferior.

A study entitled, "The Problem of Non-Attendance in Schools of the Children (6-14 years) of Scheduled Castes in Haryana" was made by Pimpley, *P.N. (1981)*, and the objectives of the study were: (i) to identify the constraints to the spread of education among the Scheduled Castes, (ii) to assess the values and attitudes of these persons with a view to finding out their effect on attendance. The findings indicated: (i) the distribution of respondents by age did not differ significantly between various sub-samples. (ii) Irrespective of caste, the spread of education among females was considerably lower than among males in the rural sample. There were more female attainders in urban area as compared to those in rural areas. (iii) Among employers, most of the children were attenders. Among those engaged in small business all were non-attenders. (iv) The educational level of the head of the household seemed to have a positive bearing upon the school attendance of children in both rural and urban samples and this was more so in the urban than in the rural sample. (v) Incidence of indebtedness was found to be significantly more wide-spread among the non-attenders. (vi) A majority of respondents felt that Scheduled Caste students were well treated in school. (vii) There was a positive relationship between awareness of reservation policy and attendance.

Lal (1985), studied the adjustment problems of scheduled caste students in schools of Haryana with special reference to some personality variables. The study was conducted on a sample of 560 students from urban and rural areas including both girls and boys. The sample consisted of male and female students of scheduled caste and general category students. Three standardized test were used for collecting the necessary information from the sampled population. The data were analyzed through a three way factorial design of the analysis of variance order. The study revealed that the general category students are more adjustable than scheduled caste students because scheduled caste students are lower than the general category people so far as their personality factor is concerned.

Khobragade, V. (1985), investigated the educational problems of post graduate scheduled caste woman students. All scheduled caste woman students taking higher education in Aurangabad city during year 1883-84 formed the sample. The total number of such students during that year was 50. All of them were interviewed and information was also collected with the help of questionnaire. The study revealed that maximum scheduled caste woman students had financial problems, low educated parents, less physical condition required for study etc. The study also showed that maximum girls scheduled caste students were taking education i) to gain status in the society ii) for gaining economic and personal independence iii) to improve one's personality iv) to progress v) to become ideal woman and vi) to gain intellectual heights. Many of the scheduled caste girls held DR. B.R. Ambedkar as their ideal.

Chauhan (1975), Yadav (1983) and *Shah (1989)*, found that the most significant reason behind the scheduled caste backwardness in education lies not in their culture but in the financial problems, poverty and non-implementation of government funds and schemes.

Singh, Kunwar. Harpal (1989), in his study of 'Personality characteristics and psycho-social problems of scheduled caste students in Rajasthan' found that, the scheduled caste students differed significantly in terms of occupational structure of parents as compared to non-scheduled caste students.

Another study by *Elangovan, P. (1989)*, reveals that, the factors related to teachers, parents, community, students, economic status and also other factors come in the way of scheduled caste education and act as barriers in many times.

Barua, A.P. (1989), studied the causes of large scale failure of scheduled caste students in the Matric (H.S.L.C.) examination in Assam. He found that, inadequate number of teachers, teachers' inefficiency in teaching, non-existence of any incentives for good teachers, inadequate school inspection, miss-appropriations of funds, pupil related causes neglected by parents are some genuine causes behind the large scale failure and backwardness of scheduled caste students in secondary level of education in Assam. He also found that all these factors are equally responsible for dropout of school children.

Chandrasekharaiah, K. (1969), studied about the educational problems of scheduled castes of Mysore. The study carried out with the following objectives—(i) to investigate into the educational problems of scheduled castes in rural and urban societies of Mysore; (ii) to examine how far school participation and school performance of the scheduled caste children were related to factors like school environment, family background and parental attitudes, and the community structure; and (iii) to examine whether the community structure and the general position of the scheduled castes in different community settings had relevance to explaining possible differences in the school performance of scheduled caste children in rural and urban areas. The major findings were reported under two main heads as school participation and school performance. The participation at the preschool stage was largely affected by the economic conditions of the family which failed to afford the expenditure involved in pre-school education and the earning foregone by the child due to schooling, and the unfavourable attitudes of the parents towards preschool education. Nearly 78.5 per cent of scheduled caste students were studying in municipal primary schools, 8 per cent in private primary schools and the rest in the government primary schools in Dharwar. The low enrolment in private primary schools was attributed to charging of fees in the form of donation, library fees, sports fees, etc., distance from the scheduled caste populated areas, frequent refusal to admission, and discriminatory treatment to the scheduled caste children. The largest number of dropouts in case of boys was in standard II and that for girls between standards II and V. the reasons for the incidence were unfavourable attitude of the scheduled caste parents towards education, low aspiration level of parents, frustrating experience of the pupils at the school, early marriage in case of girls and poor economic conditions. Girls education at the secondary level was not much favoured by their parents and the schedule caste girls were overtaken by the diverse household activities. The scheduled caste children felt ill about their dress and purchase books because of their poor economic condition and irregular and untimely government assistance. In case of school performance it was found that the percentage of detention was highest in standard I, percentage of failure among the scheduled caste pupils was highest in standard X and teachers were more optimistic about the performance of scheduled caste pupils in games and cultural activities.

A study was made by *Khobragade, V. (1985)*, on Educational Problems of Postgraduate Scheduled Caste Woman students. Some of the major findings were: (1) in a city with a population of three lakhs, there were only 50 SC girls taking post-graduate education. (2) all these girls reported that they were taking postgraduate education to get jobs. (3) major difficulties mentioned by the girls in relation to studies were absence of space for study, lack of electricity and overcrowding. (4) twenty-two girls read daily newspapers, seven read weeklies, 13 read both, while eight did not read anything. (5) thirty-nine girls had a radio in the house while 11 had no means of reaction. Five families had musical instruments in the house. (6) thirty-six girls replied that they were influenced by political leaders, 38 by social leaders, 27 by spiritual leaders, and 25 by thinkers. (7) eight girls could remember the name of one book they had read, 23 could remember two books, seven three books, 12 four books, ten did not answer the question. (8) in general, the girls reported that they were taking education. (i) to gain status in the society. (ii) for gaining economic and personal independence. (iii) to improve one's personality (iv) to progress, (v) to become ideal women, (vi) to gain intellectual heights. Many of the Sc girls held Dr. B.R. Ambedkar as their ideal.

'Problems of the scheduled caste college students of Bombay' was studied by *Chitnis, S. (1976)*. The objectives of the investigation were—(i) to study the academic position of the schedule caste students in higher education; (ii) to examine the social background of the scheduled caste students that was favourable/unfavourable to their academic life; (iii) to study the financial condition of the scheduled caste students; and, (iv) to study the scheduled caste students in comparison with the general students.

A study entitled 'Educational Problems of the Scheduled Castes in Haryana (college students)' was made by *Gangrade, K.D. (1974)*. The study was undertaken to investigate the socio-economic background of the SC college students of Haryana and to understand the educational problems of the SC students. The study aimed at investigating the changes resulting out of the constitutional provision for more facilities and economic assistance provided to them, and seeing what they felt about these facilities. The major findings of the study were as follows: (i) The students, due to certain problems inherent in their social background had not been able to take full advantage of the facilities provided by the constitution. (ii) The home environment of SC students was not found to be congenial for their development; majority of them had illiterate parents and siblings. (iii) Only one-tenth of SC students had high level of participation in extracurricular activities, two thirds had low level of participation. (iv) Only about one-tenth of them showed participation in political activities. (v) One-sixth of them complained of ill-treatment in society. (vi) Majority of the SC students were older for the classes of their study. (vii) Very few were found in science and commerce faculties. (viii) Their occupational and educational aspirations were very low.

A study entitled 'Educational problems of the Scheduled Castes in Haryana (School Students)' carried out by Gangrade, *K.D. (1974)*, keeping ahead the following objectives—(i) to assess the status of the Scheduled Caste students in the educational institutions; (ii) to compare the Scheduled caste students, wherever possible, with the non-Scheduled Caste students; and (iii) to identify the kinds of discrimination and types of difficulties and obstacles that they faced. The following were some of the major findings: (i) The Scheduled caste students of the sample were mostly Hindus by religion and Chamar by caste. (ii) In most cases both the parents were illiterate. (iii) Nearly half of the respondents had average economic condition, and one-quarter of the respondents had difficult economic condition. (iv) Parents of two-thirds of the respondents had to support others besides the respondents. (v) Educational and occupational aspirations of the Scheduled Caste students were more or less high. (vi) Most of the respondents received encouragement from their parents to get education. (vii) The Scheduled Caste students had decided about their career on their father's advice and would also care for their parents' choice in case of their marriage. (viii) A majority of the teachers considered the Scheduled Caste lower in caliber as compared to their non-Scheduled Caste peers. (ix) The policy of reservation for the Scheduled Caste was considered to be unjustified by some teachers, but supported by many for its usefulness.

STUDIES RELATED TO HIGHER EDUCATION OF SCHEDULED CASTE STUDENTS

Aikara, J.C. (1980), had conducted a study on scheduled caste and higher education, a study of college students in Bombay to find out i) the ratio of stagnation and droupout among scheduled caste students to investigate its reasons and post dropout situation ii) to understand the situation of scheduled caste college students and iii) to compare scheduled caste and non scheduled caste college students, and scheduled caste students in different colleges. In this study one one college was selected as a sample from arts, science, commerce and law run by the govt. and by the other organization and showed the following results—1) In comparison with the non SC students the scheduled caste students were found to be inferior in almost every aspect in socio economic and academic background and in performance and progress in studies. 2) The students studying in the govt. college had a superior background and better performance record than those of private colleges. 3) There had been a very high incidence of stagnation and dropout among the scheduled caste students.

Thiagargarjan (1983), conducted a study the scheduled caste students in the Madurai Kamraj University. The major objectives were—(i) to study the enrolment of scheduled caste students in the Madurai Kamraj University during the period of 1972 to 1981 with respect to certain institutional and students background variables. (ii) to identify the dropout rate and causes thereof (iii) to study the provision of incentives scheme for scheduled caste and their utilization (iv0 to study social relationship existing between scheduled caste students and caste groups and among different scheduled caste group. The revealed that—1). About 73 per cent of the general courses scheduled caste students and 66 per cent of professional course scheduled caste students were first generation learners. 2). Professional course scheduled caste students were superior to general scheduled caste students with regard to SES. 3). around 31 per cent of scheduled caste students had difficulties in comprehensing instruction through the English medium. They had special difficulties in subject like—physics, chemistry, botany, mathematics, accountancy and statistics. 4). Almost all 99.6 per cent of the students got scholarships. 5). Compensatory teaching was prevalent in general college.

Ram (1987), had conducted an analytical survey of living and study condition of scheduled caste students studying in the Baranas Hindu University. The main objectives of the study were—(i) the percentage of scheduled caste students admitted in various department of the university (ii) the socio economic status of scheduled caste students studying in the Baranas Hindu University (iii) living and study condition during students life (iv) students attitude towards education (v) problems of scheduled caste students and their opinion about the education. Three hundred students studying in the Baranas Hindu university department in the 1983-84 sessions were selected for providing data. The result of the study revealed that the study condition, living condition of scheduled caste students studying in BHU were not satisfactory.

Sharma, J.P. (1982), had conducted a research on A Study of Scheduled Caste Students in Patna University. The purpose of the study were: (i) to identify social, economic, and educational and political problems of the Scheduled Caste students studying in Patna University, and (ii) to study their relationship with teachers and students of upper caste. The main findings of the study were: (i) there was disparity between Scheduled Castes and other castes in respect of age, habitation, facilities, per capita income, parental education, study facilities, choice of subjects, rate of stagnation, adjustment to the climate in the hostel and in the institution, and level of academic achievement. (ii) immediate measures should be taken to develop confidence among the Scheduled Caste students and also for developing in them a sense of belongingness to the university system.

NIEPA (1986), studied the trends of enrolment of the scheduled caste in higher education (1964-77), New Delhi. The main objectives of the study were (i) to find out the overall trends of enrolment at the national level and the state level (ii) to analyze the overall inequality in the sphere of enrolment in higher education (iii) to trace the interstate disparities in terms of enrolment (iv) to find out the disparity between the enrolment of scheduled caste male and female and (v) to find out the level of equality achieved in different states. The major findings of the study were—1) In all the sectors of education there was a decline in the rate of growth in scheduled caste enrolment during 1972-77. In professional and other education (collegiate) there was a negative rate of growth in enrolment of scheduled caste as well as non-scheduled caste students during the period of 1972-76. 2) There were great disparities in rates of growth in enrolment of scheduled caste and non scheduled caste in the states and union territories. This disparity was more pronounced in the case of scheduled caste enrolment. 3) There was no close relationship between concentration of scheduled caste population in a particular region and its enrolment concentration. 4) The scheduled caste were still lagging far behind other communities in every stages of education and the educational disparities between scheduled caste vis-à-vis other communities become more and more acute from primarily to secondary level and from secondary to higher level of education.

STUDIES RELATED TO WASTAGE STAGNATION AND DROPOUT AMONG SCHEDULE CASTES

Kumar, V. (1983), conducted a study in order to highlight the principal reason for poor enrolment and heavy dropouts and to suggest remedial measures of the Harijan (scheduled caste) in Bihar. The study revealed that (i) enrolment and dropout rates were higher among boys than girls, (ii) a few caste e.g. Dhobi, Dusadh among the scheduled caste were more keen on education than the rest and thus showed differential development (iii) the enrolment rate was higher among the non scheduled caste whereas the dropout rate was higher among scheduled caste (iv) child education very significantly correlated with the educational status of guardians/ parents (v) the rate of dropout was more heavy at the primary stage (vi) caste discrimination in school had compounded the problem.

A critical study of non-enrolment wastage and stagnation during the first two years of primary education of scheduled caste boys and girls was carried out by Dhongade (1986). As a sample 17 villages out of 115 villages from Soyegaon Taluka were selected randomly these were divided into three. The major groups findings the study were— 1) scheduled caste and scheduled tribe population in the three types of villages were 9.78 per cent, 15.22 per cent and 31.68 per cent respectively. Scheduled caste and scheduled tribe population was more in smaller villages. 2) During the year of 1981-82 the total enrolment of SC/ST students was 40.7 per cent of non enrolment of girls was longer than that of boys. Non-enrolment was maximum in villages with a population between 1000 and 2000. 3) The economic condition of scheduled caste families, lack of parents, lack of social mobility and lack of adequate communication were the important factors coming in the way of enrolment of SC/ST. 4) The teachers in rural areas particularly in areas where scheduled caste and scheduled tribe students were in large proportion, were not effective. Many of them were untrained, lacked social awareness and enthusiasm and frequently absented themselves from school lacked minimum facilities.

Soni (1975), George (1976), Shah (1981), Chauhan (1975), and *Goyel (1992)*, have studied that both the retention and dropout of scheduled castes students in school level and college level of education are influenced by the availability, affective administration and implementation of the programmes for the welfare of the scheduled castes provided by the government and this is likely to lead the progress of their education.

CONCLUSION

The scheduled caste people are very backward in almost all the aspects of development in comparison to the non-scheduled caste people in different states of the country. Their position in education is very low almost in all the states of the country in comparison to the non-scheduled caste people in the state. Their literacy percentage is lower than the general people in all the state, their participation in education is also lower, their attitude toward education also less favourable, their intelligence level also found very lower than the general people, their academic achievement also found very low in different studies conducted by different numbers of research scholar, experts and other social workers in the respective state. So far the awareness about the education of scheduled caste parents, guardians and students are concerned, they are less aware about the education of their own and their children too, which found from various research reports. Scheduled caste people are very poor in their socio-economic conditions, and as a result the parents or guardians of the scheduled caste people usually preferred to send their kids to the different field to earn money instead of sending them to the school. This attitude of the parents and guardians of the scheduled caste affects the education of the children.

REFERENCES

Buch, M.B. Ed (1974), A Survey of Research in Education; CASE; M.S. University; Baroda.

Buch, M.B. Ed. (1979), Second Survey of Research in Education (1972-1978), Society for Educational Research and Development; Baroda.

Buch, M.B. Ed. (1987), Third Survey of Research in Education, NCERT; New Delhi.

Buch, M.B. (1991), Fourth Survey of Educational Research, (1983-88), Vol. I and II, NCERT, New Delhi.

Chalam, K.S. (1988), *Education and Weaker Sections*; Inter India Publications; New Delhi.

Chatterjee, S.K. (1996), *The Scheduled Caste in India*, Gyan Publishing House, New Delhi.

Chatterjee, S.K. (2000), *Educational Development of Scheduled Caste: Looking Ahead*, Gyan Publishing House, New Delhi.

Chitnis, S. (1974), First Survey in Social Sciences; ICSSR; New Delhi.

Chitnis, S. (1978), Education of the Scheduled Castes and Scheduled Tribes in Maharashtra, in *The Social Context of Education,* Edited by A.B. Shah, Allied Publishers, New Delhi.

Malhotra, N. and Rizvi, N. (1997), *Source Material on Education of Scheduled Castes and Scheduled Tribes*, Anamika Publishers and Distributors (P) Ltd., Delhi, p. 373.

IV

Research Approach

ANTHROPOLOGICAL RESEARCH APPROACH/ETHNOGRAPHIC RESEARCH APPROACH

Besides the approaches of research, it is quite necessary to select the method of research to be followed to carry out the research study in a smooth manner. The choice of the method of research is determined by the nature of the problems. Because of the methods apparent care and directness, descriptive method has undoubtedly been the most popular and most widely used research in education. So far as the nature and scatterdness of the data of the present study has been carried out through the descriptive survey method. The descriptive survey investigation includes such expressions as descriptive, survey, normative status, and trend. Descriptive studies may include present facts or current conditions concerning the nature of a group of persons, a number of objects or a class of events, and may involve the procedures of induction, analysis, classification, enumeration, or measurement. The term survey and status suggest the gathering of evidence relating to current conditions.

Description about Data and its Nature: It is worthwhile to mention here that data require for the present study have been collected from various sources, such as—Namasudra students studying at the secondary level, parents of those students and the community members where the selected students are belong to from the state West Bengal. Besides these, secondary data also have been collected from various sources such as—Govt. Office, Organization, Institution, Website, books, journals, News paper, periodicals, Doctoral Dissertation to fulfill the objectives or to achieve the goal of the study. A methodological diagram (Table 4.1) of the study is given below.

In order to know the present status, participation rate in education, attitudes towards education and problems faced by the Namasudra students; the researcher had to use the holistic approach of data collection from the field. Data have been collected from the different sources for qualitative and quantitative analysis and interpretation. Data required for the present research study were scattered in different ways so far as the nature of distribution of the population is concerned. The present study adopted the existing approach in educational research along with the ethnographic as well as psycho-graphic approaches. The approach adopted by the researcher in the context of collecting required data is a composite approach which can be treated as an "Anthropological approach in educational research" (the study involve educational, ethnographic and psych-graphic approach) and the frame of the study has been illustrated in the theoretical framework of the study.

Table 4.1: Methodological Description of the Study

Objectives of the study	*Description of tools/techniques*	*Sources of data*	*Nature of data*
To examine the extent of scheduled caste's participation in education in West Bengal.	Official records, Website, Census Reports, books, journals etc.	Secondary sources	Quantitative
To find out the extent of participation of Namasudra in education in West Bengal.	Official records, Website, Census Reports, books, journals etc.	Secondary sources	Quantitative
To study the attitudes of Namasudra students, Parent and Community members towards education.	Attitude scale for Namasudra students, parents and community members.	Primary sources	Quantitative and Qualitative
To study the problem faced by the Namasudra students in the secondary level of Education in West Bengal.	Questionnaire and Problem Checklist for the Namasudra students.	Primary sources	Quantitative
To make recommendations for equitable participation of different castes among SC's in Education	Researcher's Observation	Researcher's Views	Qualitative

The Target Population: In the present study all the Namasudra students studying at the secondary level of school in West Bengal,,and their parents, community members belong to Namasudra community where those selected students are living in the state constituting the target population of the present study. As the main purpose of the present study is to find out the participation level of Namasudra people, to their attitude toward education, problem faced by them in pursuing education, so the population of this category is considered as the population of the present study. The total number Namasudra population in West Bengal is 281,6202 (according to census of India 2001).

Sampling: Sampling is the process of selecting a sample from the population. It is the process through which it is possible to draw valid inferences or generalizations on the basis of careful observation of variables within a relatively small proportion of the population. In the present study purposive sampling techniques have been adopted as because the sources or populations are being scattered in the state widely; again how many students under Namasudra community are enrolled in the class IX and Class X would be very difficult to find out in the state; that is why three district from the state having more concentration of Namasudra people than the other districts have been selected randomly for the study. From each of the district 100 secondary level Namasudra students studying at Class-IX and X, 100 parents of Namasudra students and 100 Namasudra community members i.e. 100+100+100= 300 sample from each district i.e. 300 X3 = 900 sample (students-300, parents-300 and community members-300) have been selected from the state for the present study.

Sample: There are 18 districts in West Bengal. Scheduled caste populations are scattered in all the districts of West Bengal. According to census report 2001, the total number of population is 8,02,21,171 and total number of scheduled caste population is 18,452,555. Out of these the total number of Namasudra population is 281,6202. From the 18 (eighteen) number of districts three districts namely, Nadia, North 24 Paragana and Jalpaiguri have been selected for the present study. Because in this three districts concentration of Namasudra people is more than that of other districts of the state. There are 900 sample (100 from each section i.e. students, parents and community member total 300; i.e. 300 × 3 = 900) have been selected for the present study. The distribution of students, parents and community members, district wise are given below in the Table 4.2.

The total number of sample in West Bengal including the entire three districts is 300 + 300 + 300 = 900.

The total number of sample in West Bengal including the entire three districts is 300+300+300= 900.

Tools: The one of the most important prerequisite of the research process is tool. Preparation of a tool requires skill, expertness and deepest knowledge about the tool construction process. Scientifically prepared tool can ensure desired results with its proper validity and reliability. In the present study research tools were constructed on the basis of the objectives of the study. The selection of a tool for a particular study depends upon various considerations, such as the objectives of the study, the nature of data requires for the study, the time limit at the disposal of the researcher, availability of the suitable tool, materials, sources, the personal competency of the researcher to administer them etc. There are two types of tools may be used in the research process; one is the self developed or standardized tool, self prepared but not standardized and readymade standardized tool. In the present study the researcher has used two types of tools such as—self prepared and standardized tools.

Table 4.2: Sample from West Bengal

Types of Sample	*No. of Sample*		
	Nadia	*North 24 Paragana*	*Jalpaiguri*
Namasudra students	100	100	100
Namasudra parents	100	100	100
Namasudra community member	100	100	100

For the present study the researcher has prepared three standardized attitude scale such as—(i) Attitude scale on—Attitude towards education of Namasudra students, (ii) Attitude towards education of Namasudra parents, and (iii) Attitudes towards education of Namasudra Community

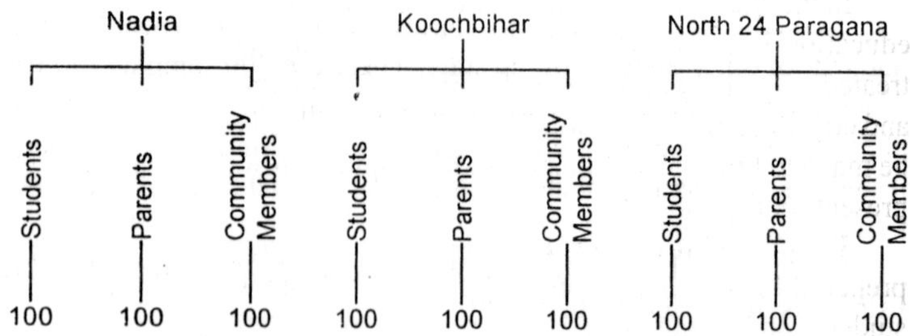

Diagrammatical Classification of Sample Taken from West Bengal

members. *Then two self prepared standardized tools are* (i) Problem Checklist for Namasudra students studying at secondary level of school, and (ii) Problem Questionnaire for secondary level Namasudra students.

Construction of Attitude Scale

An information form that attempts to measure the attitude or belief of an individual is known as an opinionnaire, or attitude scale. Because the terms opinion and attitude are not synonymous, clarification is necessary. An attitude is usually viewed as an enduring disposition to respond consistently in a given manner to various aspects of the world, including persons, events, and objects. It is a psychological factor having some similarity with traits and interest. Attitude is a reflection of personality. It may consider as a manner, mode of response of an individual towards thing, idea, person, object or a situation. Attitude is chained with stimulus in the following ways—

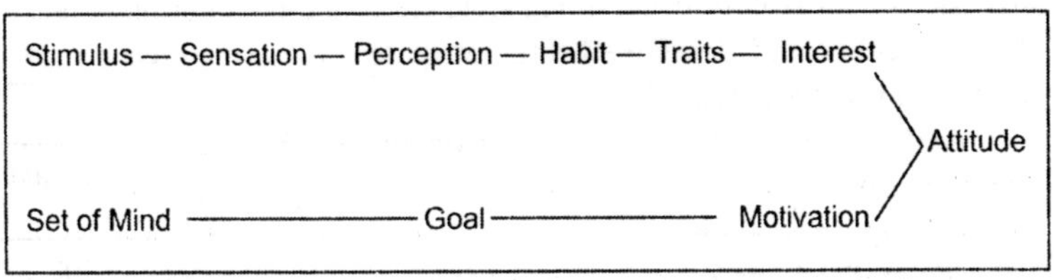

Attitude denotes—"sum total of man's inclination and feelings, prejudices or preconceived notions, ideas, fear, threats or convictions about any specific topic". Thurston (1946) defines an attitude as the degree of positive or negative affect associated with some psychological objects. By a psychological objects, he means any institution, ideal, symbol, phrase, slogan, job or idea towards which people can differ with respect to positive or negative effect.

In the study attitude denotes, perception feeling, concept, ideas about education in relation to their life. As the Namasudra people are being treated as scheduled caste and maximum of them are socio-economic and educationally backward. Therefore, through this study attempt would be made to know about their attitude or opinion towards education in the present modern society.

Purpose of the Attitude Scale: In the study attitude scale have been prepared for students belong to Namasudra community, parents of those students and Community member of the society where these people are living. To achieve the third objective of the study i.e. (to study the attitude of the Namasudra students, parents and community member) the attitude scales for all the three group people have been prepared. All the three attitude scale was developed and standardized by the researcher himself.

Emergence for Designing the Attitude Scale: After investigation thoroughly it was found that, there are good numbers of attitude scale available in the market; which are prepared for to measure various attitudes of the people such as—attitude scale for pre-school education, attitude scale for religion, attitude toward educational administration etc. but no scale was found which is prepared to measure the attitude towards education of scheduled caste in general and Namasudra people in particular. As the study confined with Namasudra and with the state of West Bengal, therefore the researcher had felt need of special attitude scale for Namasudra people in particular to know their attitude, opinion, feeling, perception about the education. Another important point is that, people those who are living basically in the North East part of India and people living in main land of the country are different so far as their attitude, social structure and living style are concerned. For these reasons the researcher had developed three attitude scales for three groups of people in the present study.

Attitude Scale Construction Procedure: There are two different popular procedures may be followed in preparing attitude scale, which are—Thurston Scale procedure and Likert method. In the present study, Likert's method has been followed for preparing the attitude scale. The Likert's method of measuring attitude in any field is somewhat easier as well as less time consuming and economical than the Thurston's scale. It is begin with some considerable number of statements of attitude toward something. They are either decidedly favourable or decidedly unfavourable about the object, institution, group of persons. Each statement usually has five possible responses.

	Weights Positive	*Weights Negative*
(i) SA (Strongly Agree)	4	0
(ii) A (Agree)	3	1
(iii) U (Undecided)	2	2
(iv) DA (Disagree)	1	3
(v) SDA (Strongly Disagree)	0	4

In the present scale, above mentioned five points scale had been used. In the scale equal number of positive and negative statements have been used, and against of each statement five points responses are also being used such as—SA, A, U, DA, SDA in all the three scales. The scoring key for the scale was also used as mentioned above. The scoring key is shown in Table 4.3.

Table 4.3: The Scoring Key for Attitude Scale

Degree of choice	*Scoring for Item's*	
	Positive	*Negative*
Strongly Agree	4	0
Agree	3	1
Undecided	2	2
Disagree	1	3
Strongly Disagree	0	4

ATTITUDE SCALE FOR NAMASUDRA STUDENTS

This attitude scale was developed by following Rensis Likert's method. Students' studying at the secondary level for them this scale has been developed. By this scale, attempts have been made to know their attitudes, perception, feeling, concept and general views regarding education. The term 'education' will carry the both broad and narrow meaning here. Education has different dimension and it has relation with every sort of elements of our life. In the present scale following 6 (six) dimensions have been taken into consideration during the preparation of the scale. They are—(i) Attitude towards education relating to society (ii) Attitude towards education relating to home or family (iii) Attitude towards education relating to school (iv) Attitude towards education relating to teacher (v) Attitude towards education relating to personal experiences (vi) Attitude towards education relating to socio-economic condition of the family. For preparing the present scale the researcher took help from various existing attitudes scale developed by different expert, had consulted with different experts, teachers, students, community members and parents of the Namasudra students. Initially the researcher prepared 140 items for the scale covering all those dimensions selected earlier having equal number of positive and negative items.

After preparing the preliminary draft scale it was sent to the experts for their recommendations, and then it was discussed among the departmental teachers. After a little modification according to expert's recommendations final draft for pilot study was prepared having 120 items, which consist of 60 positive and 60 negative statements.

After draft scale had prepared the scoring key was developed as suggested by Likert. The scoring key for positive or favourable items were decided to be 4, 3, 2, 1, 0 for responses—strongly agree (SA), agree (A), undecided (U), disagree (U), strongly disagree (SD), respectively; and for the negative or unfavourable items the scoring key was—0, 1, 2, 3, 4 strongly agree (SA), agree (A), undecided (U), disagree (U), strongly disagree (SD), respectively (Table 4.4).

Table 4.4: The Scoring Key for Attitude Scale is Shown Below—

Degree of choice	*Scoring for Item's*	
	Positive/Favourable	*Negative/Unfavourable*
Strongly Agree	4	0
Agree	3	1
Undecided	2	2
Disagree	1	3
Strongly Disagree	0	4

Pilot Study: For the pilot study the scale was administered on a group of sample consisting of 100 students studying at secondary level of school (class ix and x students) students taking from the state. After collecting the scale from the sample group, scoring was made on the basis of scoring key. Then the respondents are arranged in ascending order on the basis of score obtained by them in the scale for calculating the discriminative value of the scale.

Then for calculating discriminating power of each item, two groups of respondents were formed by taking 27 per cent students from top from the ascending order list for upper group; and 27 per cent from bottom from the list for lower group. As in the sample group 100 respondents were there; so in upper group 27 students and in lower group 27 students taken for forming the group. After forming the group, discriminative value was calculated by using following formula.

$$ULI = RU - RL \div T$$

Here, ULI stands for upper index in the discriminative value; RU stands for the number of respondents giving 'right answer' in the upper group; and RL stands for number of students giving 'right answer' in the lower group towards education.

In the present context, let the researcher make it clear that the 'right answer' means, an attempt to the positive or favourable items as 'strongly agree' and award of four (4) marks were given against such responses. Similarly, an attempt to a negative or unfavourable item as 'strongly disagree' was also considered as 'right answer' and four (4) marks were awarded to such responses.

Thus, the award of four (4) marks was given against each right answer or responses, irrespective of upper and lower group. 'T' indicates the number of respondents in the both groups.

After calculating discriminative value, the items were discarded having less discriminative value i.e. (less than 0.50), and items kept for the final draft having more discriminative value or power.

By following the above mentioned method, good number items were discarded and 48 items were kept for the final scale. In these forty eight (48) items both positive and negative items were kept equally; and these represent all the dimensions selected for the scale. From each dimension eight (8) items were selected having equal number of positive and negative statements i.e. four (4) positive and four (4) negative items from each dimension.

Reliability of the Scale: After final draft has been prepared, the scale was again administered on a group having 100 respondents 50 from each state. Then the scale collected from the respondents and then score of each respondent calculated for determining reliability of the scale by using split-half method.

Spearman Brown prophecy formula was applied for determining the reliability co-efficient of the scale.The reliability of test is 0.83.

Objectivity of the Attitude Scale: For preparing the present scale the researcher has adopted Likert's method and also followed the scoring procedure developed by him, which ensured the objectivity of the scale.

Validity of the Scale: After discussion with the expert, teachers, students, parents and community members it is ensured that the present scale possess sufficient validity. It means the present scale will serve the purpose for which it has developed. Besides this, in the process of construction of the attitude scale, the researcher ensured that the face validity, content validity and construct validity has duly been taken care of while writing and finally selecting the statements by undertaking statistical technique and expert's opinion.

Thus, the attitude scale for the Namasudra students, towards education or towards different dimensions selected for was accepted as a valid tool to measure the attitude of the Namasudra students of West Bengal.

Standardization of the Attitude Scale: The attitude scale was further standardized by re-arranging its items in a systematic way, keeping proper emphasis on each of the six different dimensions, considered for the study. The nature of the scoring system reflects the objectivity of the scale. And hence, the scale can be considered as a standard scale for measuring attitude of the Namasudra students.

Analysis of Data Obtained through the Attitude Scale: The data gathered through the attitude scale was analyzed quantitatively as well as qualitatively. Different statistical techniques which were applied to analyze and also to interpret those data are simple percentage and 't' test.

The detail procedure of the data analysis done about the data collected through the scale has been shown in the next chapter.

ATTITUDE SCALE FOR NAMASUDRA PARENTS

This attitude scale was developed by following Likert's method. Namasudra Parents, whose children are studying at the secondary level for them this scale, have been developed. By this scale attempt has been made to know their attitudes, perception, feeling, concept and general views regarding their children's education. The term 'education' will carry the both broad and narrow meaning here. Education has different dimension and it has relation with every sort of elements of our life. In the present scale following 6 (six) dimensions have been taken into consideration. They are—(i) Attitude towards education relating to society (ii) Attitude towards education relating to home or family (iii) Attitude towards education relating to school (iv) Attitude towards education relating to teacher (v) Attitude towards education relating to personal experiences (vi) Attitude towards education relating to socio-economic condition of the family. For preparing the present scale the researcher took help from various existing attitudes scale developed by different expert, had consulted with different experts, teachers, students, community members and parents. Initially the researcher prepared 130 items for the present scale covering all those dimensions selected earlier having equal number of positive and negative items.

After preparing the preliminary draft scale it was sent to the experts for their recommendations, and then it was discussed among the departmental teachers. After a little modification according to expert's recommendations final draft for pilot study was prepared having 110 items, which consist of 55 positive and 55 negative statements.

After draft scale had prepared the scoring key was developed as suggested by Likert. The scoring key for positive or favourable items were decided to be 4,3,2,1,0 for responses—strongly agree (SA), agree (A), undecided (U), disagree (U) and strongly disagree (SD) respectively; and for the negative or unfavourable items the scoring key was—0,1,2,3,4 strongly agree (SA), agree (A), undecided (U), disagree (U) and strongly disagree (SD) respectively.

Table 4.6: The Scoring Key for Attitude Scale is Shown Below—

Degree of choice	*Scoring for Item's*	
	Positive/Favourable	*Negative/Unfavourable*
Strongly Agree	4	0
Agree	3	1
Undecided	2	2
Disagree	1	3
Strongly Disagree	0	4

Pilot Study: For the pilot study the scale was administered on a group of sample consisting of 100 parents whose child studying at secondary level of school (class IX and X students) from state. After collecting the scale from the sample group, scoring was made on the basis of scoring key. Then the respondents were arranged in ascending order on the basis of marks secured by them in the scale for calculating the discriminative value of the scale.

Then for calculating discriminating power of each item, two groups of respondents were formed by taking 27 per cent students from top from the ascending order list for upper group; and 27 per cent from bottom from the list for lower group. As in the sample group 100 respondents were there; so in upper group 27 parents and in lower group 27 parents taken for forming the group. After forming the group, discriminative value was calculated by using following formula.

$$ULI = RU - RL \div T$$

Here, ULI stands for upper index in the discriminative value; RU stands for the number of respondents giving 'right answer' in the upper group; and RL stands for number of parents giving 'right answer' in the lower group towards education.

In the present context, let the researcher make it clear that the 'right answer' means, an attempt to the positive or favourable items as 'strongly agree' and award of four (4) marks were given against such responses. Similarly, an attempt to a negative or unfavourable item as 'strongly disagree' was also considered as 'right answer' and four (4) marks were awarded to such responses. Thus, the award of four (4) marks was given against each right answer or responses, irrespective of upper and lower group. 'T' indicates the number of respondents in the both groups.

After calculating discriminative value, the items were discarded having less discriminative value i.e. (less than 0.50), and items kept for the final draft having more discriminative value or power.

By following the above mentioned method, good number items were discarded and only 40 items were kept for the final scale. In these forty (40) items both positive and negative items were kept equally; and these represent all the dimensions selected for the scale. From four dimension eight (8) items; and from two dimensions four (4) items were selected having equal number of positive and negative statements.

Reliability of the Scale: After final draft has been prepared, the scale was again administered on a group having 100 respondents 50 from each state. Then the scale collected from the respondents and then score of each respondent calculated for determining reliability of the scale by using split-half method.

Spearman Brown prophecy formula was applied for determining the reliability co-efficient of the scale. The reliability of the test is 0.72.

$$r = \frac{N\Sigma XY - \Sigma X . \Sigma Y}{\sqrt{[N\Sigma X^2 - (\Sigma X)^2]\,[N\Sigma Y^2 - (\Sigma Y)^2]}}$$

Objectivity of the Attitude Scale: For preparing the present scale the researcher has adopted Likert's method and also followed the scoring procedure developed by him, which ensured the objectivity of the scale.

Validity of the Scale: After discussion with the experts, teachers, students, parents and community members it is ensured that the present scale possess sufficient validity. It means the present scale will serve the purpose for which it has been developed. Besides this, in the process of construction of the attitude scale, the researcher ensured that the face validity, content validity and construct validity has duly been taken care of while writing and finally selecting the statements by undertaking statistical technique and expert's opinion.

Thus, the attitude scale for the Namasudra parents, towards education or towards different dimensions selected for was accepted as a valid tool to measure the attitude of the Namasudra parents of West Bengal.

Standardization of the Attitude Scale: The attitude scale was further standardized by re-arranging its items in a systematic way, keeping proper emphasis on each of the six different dimensions, considered for the study. The nature of the scoring system reflects the objectivity of the scale. And hence, the scale can be considered as a standard scale for measuring attitude of the Namasudra parents' members.

Analysis of Data Obtained Through the Attitude Scale: The data gathered through the attitude scale was analyzed quantitatively and qualitatively. Different statistical techniques which are applied to analyze and also to interpret those data are simple percentage and 't' test. A detail analysis procedure of the data collected through this scale has been shown in the next chapter.

ATTITUDE FOR NAMASUDRA COMMUNITY MEMBER

This attitude scale was developed by following Rensis Likert's method. This scale has been developed for the Community member belong to Namasudra Community from the village where the selected students are belong. This scale attempt has been made to know their attitudes, perception, feeling, concept and general views regarding education. The term 'education' will carry the both broad and narrow meaning here. Education has different dimension and it has relation with every sort of elements of our life. In the present scale following 6 (six) dimensions have been taken into consideration. They are—(i) Attitude towards education relating to society (ii) Attitude towards education relating to home or family (iii) Attitude towards education relating to school (iv) Attitude towards education relating to teacher (v) Attitude towards education relating to personal experiences (vi) Attitude towards education relating to socio-economic condition of the family. For preparing the present scale the researcher took help from various existing attitudes scale developed by different experts, had consulted with different experts, teachers, students, community members and parents. Initially the researcher prepared 130 items for the scale covering all those dimensions selected earlier having equal number of positive and negative items.

After preparing the preliminary draft scale it was sent to the experts for their recommendations, and then it was discussed among the departmental teachers and supervisor. After a little modification according to expert's recommendations final draft for pilot study was prepared having 120 items, which consist of 60 positive and 60 negative statements.

After draft scale had prepared the scoring key was developed as suggested by Likert. The scoring key for positive or favourable items were decided to be 4,3,2,1,0 for responses—strongly agree (SA), agree (A), undecided (U), disagree (U) and strongly disagree (SD) respectively; and for the negative or unfavourable items the scoring key was—0,1,2,3,4 strongly agree (SA), agree (A), undecided (U), disagree (U) and strongly disagree (SD) respectively.

Table 4.7: The Scoring Key for Attitude Scale

Degree of choice	*Scoring for Items*	
	Positive/Favourable	*Negative/Unfavourable*
Strongly Agree	4	0
Agree	3	1
Undecided	2	2
Disagree	1	3
Strongly Disagree	0	4

Pilot Study: For the pilot study the scale was administered on a group of sample consisting of 100 community members from state. After collecting the scale from the sample group, scoring was made on the basis of scoring key. Then the respondents were arranged in ascending order on the basis of marks secured by them in the scale for calculating the discriminative value of the scale.

Then for calculating discriminating power of each item, two groups of respondents were formed by taking 27 per cent students from top from the ascending order list for upper group; and 27 per cent from bottom from the list for lower group. As in the sample group 100 respondents were there; so in upper group 27 community members and in lower group 27 community members taken for forming the group. After forming the group, discriminative value was calculated by using following formula.

$$ULI = RU - RL \div T$$

Here, ULI stands for upper index in the discriminative value; RU stands for the number of respondents giving 'right answer' in the upper group; and RL stands for number of community member giving 'right answer' in the lower group towards education.

In the present context, let the researcher make it clear that the 'right answer' means, an attempt to the positive or favourable items as 'strongly agree' and award of four (4) marks were given against such responses. Similarly, an attempt to a negative or unfavourable item as 'strongly disagree' was also considered as 'right answer' and four (4) marks were awarded to such responses. Thus, the award of four (4) marks was given against each right answer or responses, irrespective of upper and lower group. 'T' indicates the number of respondents in the both groups.

After calculating discriminative value, the items were discarded having less discriminative value i.e. (less than 0.50), and items kept for the final draft having more discriminative value or power.

By following above mentioned method, good numbers of items were discarded and 38 items were kept for the final scale. In these thirty eight (38) items both positive and negative items were kept equally; and these represent all the dimensions selected for the scale. From each dimension six (6) items were selected having equal number of positive and negative statements i.e. three (3) positive and three (3) negative items; and from one dimension eight (8) i.e. four (4) positive and four (4) negative items were selected.

Reliability of the Scale: After final draft had been prepared, the scale was again administered on a group having 100 respondents 50 from each state. Then the scale collected from the respondents and then score of each respondent calculated for determining reliability of the scale by using split-half method.

Spearman Brown prophecy formula was applied for determining the reliability co-efficient of the scale.

So, the Reliability of the test is 0.85.

Objectivity of the Attitude Scale: For preparing the present scale the researcher has adopted Likert's method and also followed the scoring procedure developed by him, which ensured the objectivity of the scale.

Validity of the Scale: After discussion with the experts, teachers, students, parents and community members it is ensured that the present scale possess sufficient validity. It means the present scale will serve the purpose for which it has developed. Besides this, in the process of construction of the attitude scale, the researcher ensured that the face validity, content validity and construct validity has duly been taken care of while writing and finally selecting the statements by undertaking statistical technique and expert's opinion.

Thus, the attitude scale for the Namasudra Community members, towards education or towards different dimensions selected for was accepted as a valid tool to measure the attitude of the Namasudra Community members of West Bengal.

Standardization of the Attitude Scale: The attitude scale was further standardized by re-arranging its items in a systematic way, keeping proper emphasis on each of the six different dimensions, considered for the study. The nature of the scoring system reflects the objectivity of the scale. And hence, the scale can be considered as a standard scale for measuring attitude of the Namasudra Community members.

Analysis of Data Obtained through the Attitude Scale: The data gathered through the attitude scale was analyzed quantitatively and qualitatively. Different statistical techniques which were applied to analyze and also to interpret those data are simple percentage and correlation. The detail analysis and interpretation process of the data collected through the scale may be perused in the next chapter.

QUESTIONNAIRE FOR STUDYING THE PROBLEM FACED BY THE NAMASUDRA STUDENTS

Questionnaire is a tool which consists of numbers of questions relating to the problem selected for research, sending to the sample for seeking answers of those questions. The terms questionnaire and schedule may be considered equivalent for present purposes, although sometimes a technical distinction is made. The questionnaire is generally regarded as a form distributed through the mail or filled out by the respondent under the supervision of the investigator or interviewer, whereas the schedule is a form filled out by the investigator or completed in his presence. It is a tool, basically descriptive in nature, which claims to pool the data—qualitative and quantitative as well, regarding the problems of a certain group of people or of an individual.

Purpose of the Questionnaire: In the present study, one of the most important objectives is to identify the problems faced by the Namasudra students in West Bengal in the process of education. To study their existing problems in the field of education relating to home, school, teacher, society, study and problem in general at the secondary level of school by the Namasudra students in West Bengal; the present tool has been developed by the researcher.

Emergence for Designing the Questionnaire: There are good numbers of questionnaire tool available in the field of education and psychology; but, no tool has been found to study the problem faced by the Namasudra students at the secondary level of school in West Bengal. That is why, the present researcher had felt need to develop a new questionnaire to fit the present objective of the study. The present researcher has developed the present tool with consultation of existing questionnaire developed by different expert in the field of educational research, and with the supervisor and experts. To explore the problems faced by the Namasudra students in West Bengal; in the field of education relating to home, school, teacher, society, study and problem in general at the secondary level, the present tool has been developed by the researcher.

Construction Procedure: In questionnaire construction important decisions related to motivation of the respondent, significance of questions, simplicity of responses, avoidance of unnecessary specifications or details, pertinence to the situation of the respondent, clarity of purpose and questions, phrasing of items to facilitate summarization of responses, and possible pre-coding of the questionnaire in the interest of using tabulating machine cards for summarization. To construct the present tool, five (5) dimensions were specified, which may be considered as component of the present scale. The categorizations of dimensions of the tool have been selected on the basis of nature of the problem faced by them at the secondary level in both the state. The dimensions of the tool may mentioned in the following ways—

i) Problem related to School
ii) Problem related to Teachers
iii) Problem related to Society
iv) Problem related to Reading
v) Genera problem related to Education Process.

Though the above mentioned dimensions of tool have been identified, still some dimension or components have remained unidentified in the present tool due to number of reason. Because, above mentioned dimensions are found very frequently and common in the problem list faced by the Namasudra students in West Bengal.

Keeping ahead the objective of the study, the researcher had prepared hundred (100) items, twenty (20) from each dimension at the beginning. In the present scale, some items were prepared with having just Yes/No responses; and in some specific cases some items were prepared having multiple responses.

Pilot Study: Before pilot study, the draft tool was sent to the experts for their comment; and it was discussed with the teachers to modify the items. After getting comments and suggestions from the teachers and experts, the researcher discarded some items and made the final draft consisting of sixty (60) items, with consultation to the supervisor. For pilot study of the tool, sample was taken the state comprising 100 respondents from the state. Then the tool was administered on the sample group thrice, and the number of items were reduced several times, and finally the number stood up to forty (40) in the final draft of the questionnaire.

Reliability and Objectivity of the Questionnaire: The data obtained by the draft questionnaire was both quantitative as well as qualitative.

The reliability or consistency of the tool was observed during the administration of the tool on the sample group. When the tool administered thrice on the sample group, the obtained by it was checked and no differences was found, from this it is inferred that the reliability of the tool sufficiently possess. Though a little fluctuation was observed in the obtained data, which was due to the number of items; but in final draft sufficient reliability was observed when it was re-administered on the sample group.

Quantitative data analysis is ensured the objectivity of the questionnaire whereas; both qualitative and quantitative data analysis ensured the reliability of the questionnaire to a great extent. In the process of ensuring the consistency of the responses towards the items of the questionnaire, valuable opinions from the experts from Namasudra community and also form the eminent educationists from the field of scheduled caste studies, were taken into consideration which ensured the researcher about the reliability of the tool.

Validity of the Questionnaire: Validity of the tool was guaranteed by the method of content and face validity. The pattern of the questionnaire revealed its face validity. When the experts analyzed the item in details than content validity was found. Because all the items represents all the dimensions selected for it.

Besides this in every phase of analyzing the items during repetitive try-out, the logical validity of the questionnaire was gained by checking the items because the units, questions incorporated in the questionnaire are directly concerned with the conceptions and components of the problems—for which the questionnaire is intended to measure. Problems identified by the questionnaire, also observed among the Namasudra students at secondary level education in both state later, which ensured the predictive validity of the questionnaire.

So, it is found that the questionnaire for the Namasudra students studying at secondary level school, as it was developed ensuring its face validity, content validity, logical validity and predictive validity.

Standardization of the Questionnaire: The questionnaire was further standardized by re-arranging the items in a systematic way, with a view to the dimensions identified and objectives of the study.

Analysis of the Data Obtained through the Questionnaire: Both quantitative as well as qualitative analysis is being made in the data obtained through the questionnaire. The data obtained through the objective questions was analyzed, without allotting any numerical score toward. them. The data obtained through multiple choice items were analyzed through quantitative and qualitative way. The data obtained through the tool has been analyzed and interpreted systematically by using statistical method such as percentage and through graphical representation which may be perused in the fifth chapter.

PROBLEM CHECKLIST FOR STUDY THE PROBLEMS FACED BY THE NAMASUDRA STUDENTS

Checklist is a selected list of words, phrases, sentences or paragraphs following which an observer records a check () to denote the presence or absence of whatever is being observed. The checklist may include items which represent expected desirable or undesirable forms of behaviour, a sequence of skills associated with a given operation, or a group of ideas. Problem checklist is a device to check the problem faced by the subjects(s) in a specified field.

Purpose of the Problem Checklist: To achieve the objective of the study; to identify the problems faced by the Namasudra students in West Bengal with regard to education, the present problem checklist has been developed.

Construction Procedure: Before constructing the problem checklist, the researcher had gone through various related literature to know the nature of the problem of scheduled caste students at secondary school in West Bengal. Besides this, the researcher consulted with some students, teachers, experts, self observation, parents, and community members etc to know the nature of the problems and to realize the problems faced by the Namasudra people in secondary level school. After having consultation with the various sources the researcher initially identified some dimensions, to which the problems are related. Then seventy (70) problem statements were prepared by the researcher. Then the draft tool was discussed with the experts, teachers and supervisor, to make sufficient modification; and consequently another more ten (10) problems were included so, it became eighty (80) and few of previous statements were modified, to avoid commonness of the problems. Problem statements were arranged in such a way that, the respondents could give their response or they could checkout the problems which they frequently and rarely faced in their study life.

After preparing the draft tool, it was administered on a group of sample having 100 respondent from the state and they were requested to check out the problems which they faced very common, sometime and very rare in their study life. In this way the tool tries out thrice and to some extent modified, and it is observed that out of eighty (80) statements the respondent gave response properly to thirty one (31) statements. So, for the final tool thirty one (31) statements were kept and rest of forty nine (49) statements were deleted from the tool; and final tool were prepared.

Reliability and Objectivity of the Problem Checklist: Data gathered by the problem checklist was quantitative in nature, and no difference was found in the data, in first and second try out of the draft checklist. So, it's ensured that data gathered by this tool from the sample has consistency, which confirmed the reliability of the tool. Besides this, suggestions, comments obtained by the tool also ensured the reliability of the tool.

The construction procedure and the nature of this data gathering tool itself ensure objectivity of the problem checklist tool.

Validity of the Problem Checklist: After discussion with the expert, teachers, students, parents and community members it is ensured that the present tool possess sufficient validity. It means the present tool will serve the purpose for which it has developed. The present tool revealed face validity, content validity, logical validity and predictive validity. The pattern of checklist revealed its face validity so far the purpose of the tool is concerned. Logical validity was gained when the individual item was analyzed, during the repetitive administration. The predictive validity of the problem checklist was ensured through the process of comparing the data obtained from some of the respondents and observing their practical life situations. Besides these, validity of the tool also gained from the expert's comments regarding the problem checklist. The experts expressed their satisfaction so far the validity of the content of the final form of the problem checklist is concerned.

Standardization of the Problem Checklist: After try out the tool, the statements of the tool were re-arranged systematically, and enough scope was given to the respondents to specify the problem in the last phase of the checklist, which ensured the standardization of the tool.

Analysis of Data Obtained through the Problem Checklist: Data obtained by the problem checklist is quantitative in nature. So, a statistical technique was applied to analyze the quantitative data such as percentage. Detail analysis procedure has been given in the next chapter.

In the present chapter the researcher has attempted to discuss the methodology adopted for the present study. In the present research study ethnographic research approaches have adopted and for which necessary tools and techniques have been developed by the researcher himself. There are five research tools have been developed for the study they are—(i) Attitude scale on—Attitude towards education of Namasudra students, (ii) Attitude towards education of Namasudra parents, and (iii) Attitudes towards education of Namasudra Community members. Then two self prepared standardized tools are (i) Problem Checklist for Namasudra students studying at secondary level of school, and (ii) Problem Questionnaire for secondary level Namasudra students. Detail descriptions about the tool construction procedure, standardization process, reliability, validity and method of application have been discussed in detail in the present chapter. The data collected through these tools and techniques have rationally analyzed and interpreted in the next chapter.

REFERENCES

Best, J.W. (1982), *Research in Education*; Prentice Hall of India Pvt. Ltd.; New Delhi.

Campbell, W.G. (1969), *Form and Style of Thesis Writing*; Houghton Mifflin Company; Boston.

Ebel, R.L. (Ed.) (1969), *Encyclopedia of Educational Research*; The Macmillan Co.; London.

Edwards, A.L. (1957), *Techniques of Attitude Scale Construction*; Appleton Century Crofts; Inc; New York.

Festinger, L. *et al.* (1970), *Research Methods in Behavioural Sciences*; Amerind Publishing Co. Pvt. Ltd; New Delhi.

Fox, D.J. (1969), *The Research Process in Education*; Holt Rinehart and Winston; New York.

Freeman, F.S. (1965), *Theory and Practice of Psychological Testing*; Oxford IBH Publishing Co.; New Delhi.

Freeman, F.S. (1971), *Theory and Practice of Psychological Testing*; (3rd Indian Edition), IBH Publishing Co.; Bombay.

Garrett, H.E. (1962), *Statistics in Psychology and Education*; Allied Pacific Private Ltd.; Bombay.

Ghurye, G.S. (1996), *Caste and Race in India*, Popular Prakashan, Bombay.

Good, C.V. Ed. (1959), *Dictionary of Education*; Mc Graw Hill Book Company; New York.

Good, C.V. *et al.* (1941), *Methodology of Educational Research*; Appleton-Century Crofts Inc.; New York.

Good, W.J. *et al.* (1952), *Methods in Social Research*, Mc. Graw Hill Book Company; New York.

Kulashrestha, S.P. (1979), *Educational Psychology*; International Publishing House; Meerut; U.P.

Kundu, C.L. (1976), *Educational Psychology*; Sterling Publishers Pvt. Ltd., New Delhi.

V

Participation of Scheduled Castes in Education

Analysis and interpretation of data is an indispensable part of any kind of research. It would be meaningless for the research if the collected data would not analyze and interpreted properly.

The type of data analysis and interpretation is depending upon the nature of data. There are two types of data analysis generally used in the educational researches viz. qualitative and quantitative analysis. In the present research work data have been analyzed through both quantitative as well as qualitative approaches. Quantitative analysis is concerned with the 'raw data' or numbers. On the other hand qualitative analysis concerned with the facts, information, possibly visual materials such as photos etc. So far the data in the study is concerned both kind of data i.e. score, numbers and facts, information are involved in the study.

DEVELOPMENT OF EDUCATION AMONG SCHEDULED CASTE IN WEST BENGAL

Choudhari and Pal (1997) examined that in the field of formal education, number of literate persons among the scheduled caste communities are still quite low in comparison to non-scheduled population, which is more significant in case of scheduled tribe communities. Considering the facts, special emphasis has been given on education sector from the very First Five Year Plan Period. Various schemes were/are extended for these two sectors of scheduled population to make an improvement over their backwardness in this important field of development i.e. education. Schools are opened in the areas where the scheduled populations live in concentration. Hostel facilities are also extended so that students and children who live in remote areas and do not get proper atmosphere for studying in their residence may get an opportunity to continue their studies in a situation where they can read with the other students of different communities.

Accordingly, Backward Classes Welfare Department of the State government provides fund for various educational schemes meant for the students of these two sectors of population.

It is also a fact that at the time of independence, the difference of literacy rates between the scheduled tribes and scheduled castes and the non-scheduled population was quite high. For the said reason, education sector received highest priority from the very First Five Year Plan Period. But the progress had never been achieved up to the desired level because of manifold reasons. Every society or community has its own tradition and cultural values, so acceptance or rejection of any innovation depends in that complex socio-cultural matrix. The planners and academicians may think that for all round development education is the key factor but to agriculture based traditional society; the people give more priority to land and agriculture development than education. Thus, if the Government wishes to make a progress and all efforts are made to increase the number of literates, achievement may not be made to the desired extent within a stipulated or target period of time. This does not mean that no progress has been made so far even after four decades. If one examines the Census Reports one may observe a significant change in this field of education.

The Scheduled Castes in West Bengal cover about 23.00 per cent (1,84,52,555) according to the Census 2001 of India to the population of the state. In 1981 they shared 21.99 per cent and in 1991, 23.62 per cent to the total population of the state. The percentage of literates among the scheduled castes of West Bengal 2001 census is 59.04 per cent, whereas

Table 5.1: Development of Education among Scheduled Caste and General People in West Bengal and India

Year	*West Bengal*	*West Bengal*	*India*	*India*
	SC WB	*GEN WB*	*SC IND*	*GEN IND*
1961	13.58	34.46	10.27	28.3
1971	17.8	38.86	14.67	34.45
1981	24.42	48.65	21.38	42.57
1991	42.21	57.7	37.41	52.21
2001	59.04	68.64	54.69	65.38
2011*	*68.24	71.64	*63.89	74.04

* Projected data.

Source: Census reports of India from 1961-2011.

the said percentages were 42.21 per cent in 1991, 24.42 per cent in 1981, 17.80 per cent in 1971 and 13.58 per cent in 1961.

From Table 5.1 it is revealed that scheduled caste of West Bengal are being educated day by day, and their literacy rate also being increasing so far their literacy rate found in various census reports are concerned. But the growth rate of scheduled caste in education is lower than the general people's participation in education in the state. It is found from the above report that according to census 1961 scheduled caste literacy in the state was 13.58 per cent, but general people's literacy rate was 34.46 per cent in the same year. In the same way scheduled caste literacy rate was being increased in various census reports of the state; but in every census it is found that their literacy percentage is lower than the general people's literacy percentage. Thus, the literacy percentage is recorded for scheduled caste people in the state is 68.24 per cent and 71.64 per cent for general people in the census 2011 in the state. So, it may be observed that schedule caste people in the state are very backward in education in comparison to the general people.

Again, it is observed from the above report that participation of scheduled caste in education in the state is better than the national level participation in education of scheduled caste people. It is found that according to the census 1961 scheduled caste literacy was 13.58 per cent and all India level scheduled caste literacy rate was only 10.27 per cent, again in 1971 SCs literacy rate 17.8 per cent and all India level SCs literacy rate 14.67 per cent. In this way it is observed from the various censuses that scheduled caste's participation in education in the state is better than the national level participation of scheduled caste in education. It is found from the above report that according to the census 2011 schedule caste literacy of the West Bengal state is 68.24 per cent and national level scheduled caste literacy rate is 63.89 per cent.

Comparative growth of Scheduled caste and general people's participation in education in the state West Bengal and India may be better understood from the histogram (Fig. 5.1).

The above mentioned graph has shown the comparative growth and development of scheduled caste and general people (overall) literacy rate in west Bengal from 1961-2011.

Enrollment status of the scheduled caste is recorded by NCERT report in 2001 that the scheduled caste people enrollment is found well at the primary level and at the higher secondary level, but in the middle levels i.e. such as in secondary level the enrollment of the scheduled caste peoples are found less in the year 2001. A detail enrollment of scheduled caste

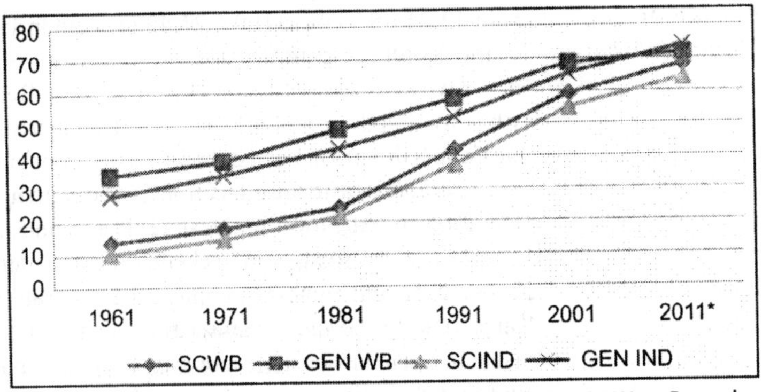

Fig. 5.1: Comparative Growth of SC and GEN in Education in West Bengal and India

students in various classes from class I-XII in rural and urban areas of the state is shown below of the state—

According to the Table 5.2 it is found that out of 23.02 per cent of scheduled caste people 26.88 per cent scheduled caste people are living in the rural areas of the state and only 13.05 per cent SCs people are living at the urban areas of the state. It is again found that in rural area 30.42 per cent of scheduled caste people enrolled their name at primary level i.e. classes I-IV. But in urban areas only 19.76 per cent of SCs students enrolled in that class and in total it becomes 28.42 per cent of scheduled caste students enrolled at the primary level of school. It implies that participation of scheduled caste population in education is found more in the rural area than the urban areas.

Table 5.2: Percentage of Scheduled Caste Enrollment in Various Classes as per 2001 in West Bengal

Area	*% of SC in total population*	*I-V*	*VI-VIII*	*IX-X*	*XI-XII*	*I-XII*
Rural	26.88	30.42	26.88	24.61	21.04	28.98
Urban	13.05	19.76	16.53	13.64	11.83	17.3
Total	23.02	28.42	23.84	20.62	16.3	26.16

Source: Seventh All India School Education Survey (7th AISES), NCERT, 2006.

Again it is found from the above table that the number of enrollment of scheduled caste students in the classes VI-VIII is 26.88 per cent in the rural areas, but only 16.53 per cent in urban areas. The most important period of secondary education is Class IX-X, in this period also it is observed from the table that the enrollment of rural scheduled caste people is found more than the urban areas. During this period the enrollment percentage of scheduled caste people is recorded in rural areas is 24.61 per cent and in urban areas only 13.64 per cent, which is around 50 per cent less than the rural area scheduled caste people.

Again it is found from the table that in the class XI-XII, the scheduled caste enrollment is total 16.3 per cent, out of which 21.04 per cent are rural people and 11.83 per cent in urban areas people. So, again it is proved that in the state West Bengal rural scheduled caste people are more involved in education than the urban areas people.

Now, if we see the enrollment of scheduled caste people in the classes from I-XII, than we find that in these classes total 26.16 per cent students are enrolled in the year 2001, and out of which 28.98 per cent are from rural and 17.3 per cent from the urban areas of the state. Overall it is found from the table that participation level of rural scheduled caste peoples are found far better than the urban areas scheduled caste people.

The enrolment of scheduled caste people in different classes in 2001 of West Bengal may be graphically shown in the Fig. 5.2.

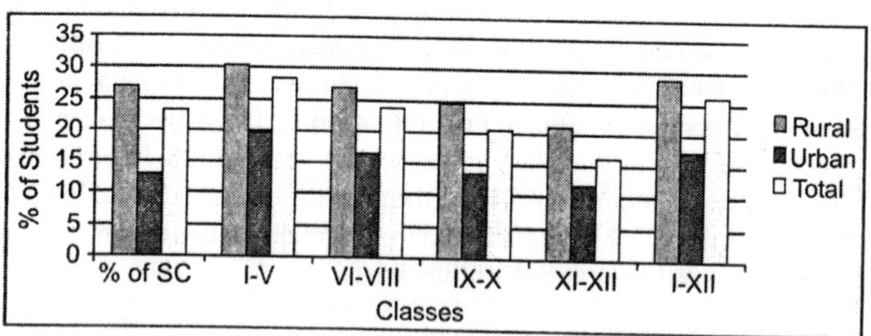

Fig. 5.2: Graphical Representation of Scheduled Caste Enrolment in Different Classes of West Bengal in 2001

The percentage of scheduled caste of different districts of West Bengal varies from census to census. There are eighteen (18) districts in West Bengal and in all the districts contained huge numbers of scheduled caste population; but their development in the field of education varies from district to district. Development of education among scheduled caste in different district of West Bengal in different years may be observed from (Table 5.3).

The above mentioned table reveals that the development of education among scheduled caste is different in various years of West Bengal. Out of eighteen districts North 24 Paragana, Kolkata and Koch Bihar possess

Table 5.3: Literacy Rate of Scheduled Castes in West Bengal: 1961-2011

Sl. No.	*State/Districts*	*1961*	*1971*	*1981*	*1991*	*2001*	*2011**
1.	West Bengal	13.58	17.80	24.42	42.21	59.04	68.24
2.	Koch Bihar	17.18	18.28	25.21	41.07	66.30	75.50
3.	Jalpaiguri	9.77	16.86	23.05	41.34	61.87	71.07
4.	Darjeeling	22.24	24.71	31.77	46.30	62.43	71.63
5.	Uttar Dinajpur	10.84	15.91	20.03	33.05	50.06	59.26
6.	Daxin Dinajpur	–	–	–	–	54.55	63.75
7.	Maldah	10.51	13.49	20.41	33.89	51.17	60.37
8.	Murshidabad	8.81	11.47	17.07	32.79	48.91	58.11
9.	Nadia	16.76	21.27	27.51	45.32	63.09	72.29
10.	North 24 Paragana	19.01	26.08	33.28	53.51	70.79	79.99
11.	South 24 Paragana	–	–	–	49.79	59.01	68.31
12.	Kolkata	28.07	31.64	42.59	56.53	70.54	79.74
13.	Haora	16.22	25.67	28.80	44.87	61.13	70.33
14.	Hugli	11.80	13.21	22.50	40.66	56.10	65.30
15.	Medinipur	14.90	19.50	26.76	54.56	63.57	72.77
16.	Bankura	7.20	10.09	14.93	29.96	42.92	52.12
17.	Puruliya	7.05	10.41	18.46	31.81	45.15	54.35
18.	Burdhwan	9.77	11.35	15.79	36.57	51.99	61.19
19.	Birbhum	7.32	10.13	14.79	27.66	45.74	54.94

*Projected data.

Source: Census reports of India, RGI, 1961-2001.

highest literacy rate such as—79.99 per cent, 79.74 per cent and 75.50 per cent respectively according to the census 2011; and lowest literacy rate possess the districts like—Bankura, Puruliya and Birbhum with the percentage 52.12 per cent, 54.35 per cent and 54.94 per cent respectively. In 2001 also the following districts such as—North 24 Paragana, Kolkata and Koch Bihar possess highest literacy rate such as—70.79 per cent, 70.54 per cent and 66.30 per cent respectively; and lowest literacy rate possess the districts like—Bankura, Puruliya and Birbhum with the percentage 42.92 per cent, 45.15 per cent and 45.74 per cent respectively. Again in the census 1991 the districts possess highest literacy rate was Kolkata, Medinipur and North 24 Paragana with the literacy rate-56.53 per cent, 54.56 per cent and 53.51 per cent respectively; and lowest literacy rate was found in the districts Birbhum, Bankura and Puruliya with the literacy rate 27.66 per cent, 29.96 per cent and 31.81 per cent respectively. From the report it is found that the districts Bankura, Birbhum and Puruliya could not achieve much in the field of education by the scheduled caste population in both the census period. It is also found from the various reports that out of 18 districts nine (9) districts lies above the measuring line, these districts are—Koch Bihar, Jalpaiguri, Kolkata, North 24 Paragana, South 24 Paragana, Darjeeling, Naida, Haora and Medinapur; and rest of the districts are lying the below measuring line.

Regarding the development of scheduled caste education U.K. Ray and M.K. Choudhari (1997) expressed that the literacy rate of scheduled caste in West Bengal has increased during last decade, though the difference compared to non-scheduled caste communities is yet to be minimized. Here it may be stated that due to Total Literacy Programme a large section of the communities came under the fold of new literates. Above all, State Government also extended number of programmes including facility of hostels for both boys and girls reading from Class V to X and special Merit Scholarship for both boys and girls reading from class IX to XII for the educational development of the state.

If we analyze the progress of education census wise of different districts than the rate of progress of scheduled caste people in education may be observed. District wise development of education among scheduled caste group is analyzed in the following paragraph. Analysis has been made here with a view to the table shown in the Chapter-II table 5.5 District Wise distribution on scheduled caste population of West Bengal from 1951-2011.

The district Koch Bihar comprise the highest number of scheduled caste population according to census 2001 i.e. 50.13 per cent in its total population. It is reveal from the above table that the SCs of this district are very much progressive in the field of education in comparison to the other districts. It is found that the number of scheduled caste population in the district has been increasing day by day; in 1951 their population was only 40.15 per cent and in 2001 it is increased up to 50.13 per cent. In the same way the participation of scheduled caste in education also increasing day by day; in 1961 their participation rate was 17.18 per cent than it was increased up to 18.28 per cent in 1971, 25.21 per cent in 1981, 41.07 per cent in 1991, in 2001 it stood up to 66.30 per cent, and in 2011 their literacy rate is observed as 75.50 per cent which is more than the state level participation rate i.e. 68.24 per cent of scheduled caste in education. It is also observed from the table that in all the mentioned above censuses scheduled caste participation rate in education was higher than the state level general people participation in education except the census 1991, in this year their literacy percentage was lower than the state level literacy percentage.

Jalpaiguri is also a scheduled caste concentrated district where 36.68 per cent of scheduled caste people are living as per 2001 census in the district. Their number of population also day by day increased except the census 2001, in this census their number of population have been decreased from 36.99 per cent to 36.68 per cent. The scheduled castes of Jalpaiguri district are not very generous towards their education and as a result their literacy rate is found low in comparison to the state level literacy rate among scheduled caste in the district. It is reported by the above table that in 1961 census their literacy rate was only 9.77 per cent, than it was increased up to 16.86 per cent in the next census, 23.05 per cent in 1981 and 41.34 per cent in 1991 census of the state. Observation declared that in all the censuses their literacy performance was lower than the state level literacy performance, but exceptionally in the census 2001 and 2011 their academic performance slightly improve to some extent above than the state SCs literacy. In this census their literacy rate stood up to 61.87 per cent and 71.07 per cent respectively in the district, whereas state SCs literacy is 59.04 per cent and 68.24 per cent.

The report declared that the concentration of scheduled caste people in Darjeeling district is low, it comprises only 16.12 per cent scheduled caste population to the total population of the district. Their population increased a lot from 1961 to 2001. It is found that in 1961 their proportion was only 5.86 per cent and in 2001 it became 16.12 per cent. It is very important to mention here is that wherever the number of scheduled caste is less there their performance in education is high. The district Darjeeling is not exception of this. In this district their number of population is less but their participation in education is higher than the state level participation of SCs in education. It is reported by the above mention table that in the census 1961 their literacy percentage was 22.24 per cent, which was too high than the state level performance. In the same way literacy rate had been increasing and finally they stood up to 71.63 per cent in the year 2011.

South Dinajpur and North Dinajpur was a single district up to 1991 census of the state. Whatever percentage of population is shown in the report up to 1991 census which is for single district, thereafter the district was divided into two separate districts such as—North Dinajpur and South Dinajpur district. It is found from the report that in both the districts percentage of scheduled caste population almost equal which is 27.70 per cent SCs in North Dinajpur and 28.79 per cent in South Dinajpur according to 2001 report. In case of literacy or participation in education also whatever percentage of literacy is shown in the above table, which is up to 1991 census for the single district. But in 2001 and 2011 literacy of both the district is shown separately, where it is found that in both the district having low literacy performance North Dinajpur 50.06 per cent and 59.26 per cent and South Dinajpur 54.55 per cent and 63.75 per cent respectively in comparison to the state level literacy performance of the SCs.

The district Maldah is having 16.84 per cent scheduled caste population with the total population. In comparison to the other district the growth rate of scheduled caste population is very slow. In the field of education also their participation level also lower than the state level participation. It is noted in the above mention table that in all the censuses their position is below than the state level position.

In the district Mursidabad number of scheduled caste population is marginal. The district is having only 12.00 per cent scheduled caste population in its total population. It is very important to mention here is that the number of scheduled caste population is decreasing day by day. If we see the census 2001 (shown in the chapter-II), than it is found that the number of SCs is decreased. In the pasture of education also the performance of SCs in education is very outrageous. It is proclaimed by the above chart that in 1961 the literacy performance of the scheduled caste population only 8.81 per cent, whereas state level literacy was 13.58 per cent; again in 2001 it increased up to only 48.91 per cent whereas state level literacy performance is 59.04 per cent that too higher than this district performance. In 2011 census their literacy percentage is recorded as 58.11 per cent against the 68.24 per cent state literacy of SCs.

The district Nadia is very sound in the field of education so far their literacy rate is concerned. It is noticed from the above table that in each census of the state brought it to light that scheduled castes of this district are more advanced in education. Though the district covers maximum rural population in its areas, still the SCs shows the high literacy than the state level scheduled caste literacy rate. According to the census 1961 their participation rate in education was 16.76 per cent, in 1971 they increased their literacy up to 21.27 per cent, in 1981 27.51 per cent, in 1991 45.32 per cent and in the latest 2001and 2011 they raised their literacy percentage up to 63.09 per cent and 72.29 per cent respectively. It is also observed from the table that in all the censuses the scheduled caste literacy rate is seen above than the state level literacy performance.

The participation of scheduled caste in education is found highest in the district North 24 Paragana of the state. But their population in the district is low than many other district of the state. Another important point is noticed here is that the number of scheduled caste population is decreasing in the district at a snail's pace. The position of scheduled caste population in the district is very far-fetched. It is notice from the various censuses that the number of SCs population in the district was 22.86 per cent in 1951, than it was increased up to 24.28 per cent in 1961, again it was decreased in 1971 into 22.61 per cent, and again it was increased up to 25.04 per cent in 1981, than their number again fall down into 21.49 per cent and gradually their number of population is found falling down in the census 2001 also, in this census their number of population is found only 20.60 per cent which very low in comparison to the earlier censuses. But their development of education is found in opposite direction. Growth of education among scheduled caste in district is found outstanding. The above table expressed that in 1961 their literacy rate was only 19.01 per cent which is more than state level performance, than it was increased up to 26.08 per cent in 1971, again 33.28 per cent in 1981, in 1991 census their performance in education was increased up to 53.51 per cent and 70.79 per cent of literacy is observed in 2001 census which is too high than the state level scheduled caste literacy performance. Again in 2011 census also their performance is observed as 79.99 per cent which is quite better than many other districts. It also noticed from the above table that their performance is found higher than state level performance in each census.

South 24 Paragana district and North 24 Paragana district was the single district before 1991 census report of the state. So, separate census is noticed of the district from 1991 census of the state. The number of scheduled caste population is higher than the North 24 Paragana district so far the census report 1991 and 2001 is concerned. It is observed from the census that in this district 32.10 per cent scheduled caste population are living whereas in North 24 Paragana only 20.60 per cent SCs are found. But literacy percentage of South 24 Paragana is only 68.21 per cent according to 2011 census, whereas in North 24 Paragana is 79.99 per cent in the same census. So, it may be conclude that scheduled castes living in the district are not as conscious as North 24 Paragana district's Scheduled caste towards their education.

Kolkata is the capital district of the state, which comprises marginal number (6%) of scheduled caste population in the total population of the district. As the present district is the capital district so, literacy percentage of the people would be higher than any other district of the state. It is observed from the above table that in each census of the district, scheduled caste participation in education is found higher than any other district of the state. It implies that the district might have provided all sorts of facilities of accessing education to the all people living in the district. It has already been mentioned that wherever the number of scheduled caste population is found less there educational development is found very sound than the district where scheduled caste population is higher. It is reported from the above table that in the census 1961 scheduled caste people literacy was 28.07 per cent which is more than double than the state level literacy performance. Again if we see the pace of progress of scheduled caste people in education than the above table again it expresses that in 1971 their literacy rate was 31.64 per cent, in 1981 it became 42.59 per cent, in 1991 it stood up to 56.53 per cent and in 2001 their literacy stood up to 70.54 per cent and finally in 2011 the district recorded highest level literacy rate that is 79.74 per cent.

Howrah district comprises 15.41 per cent of scheduled caste population according to 2001 census of the state. This district also has good number of educated scheduled caste population in its total population. And their rate of progress in education is also up to the mark. Highest rate of progress in education is seen during 1981-1991 period. In 1981 the district had literacy rate 28.80 per cent, but all of a sudden it increased up to 44.87 per cent in the year of 1991. Again in the year 2001 scheduled caste people in the district progressed in the field of education up to 61.13 per cent. And finally the district recorded as 70.33 per cent in 2011 census.

23.58 per cent of scheduled caste population are found in the district Hugli in the year 2001 but their rate of participation in education is found in the 2011 year is only 65.30 per cent. It is seen from the above table that from the very earlier time the district had low literacy percentage among scheduled caste people in comparison to the all people literacy performance. In 1961 the district had 11.80 per cent of literate scheduled caste people in its total population which was lower than the state level scheduled caste literacy performance.

Medinapur is a developed district in comparison to the other district of the state. It comprises 16.35 per cent of scheduled caste population with its total population. As it is a developed district so, it is developed in all sides. So far their educational development is concerned the district position is fourth i.e. percentage of literacy of the scheduled caste people is 72.77 per cent in 2011. It is reported by the above table that in all the censuses the district has higher scheduled caste literacy in comparison to the state level scheduled caste literacy.

Marginal literacy percentage is found in the districts Bankura, Puruliya and Birbhum. The Bankura comprises good number of scheduled caste i.e. 31.24 per cent in its total population according to the census 2001 but, this is the district which has lowest scheduled caste participation in education i.e. 52.12 per cent out of all the districts of the state as per 2011 census. In the same way Puruliya and Birbhum district also carries marginal literacy among scheduled caste people i.e. 54.35 per cent and 54.94 per cent as per 2011 census. All the three districts had very subsidiary number of literate scheduled caste population in the year 1961, such as Bankura 7.20 per cent, Puruliya 7.05 per cent and Birbhum 7.32 per cent. Again it is seen from the table that their growth rate in education is very slow, and all the three districts had almost same pace of progress in the field of education. It is observed from the table that in 1971 all the three had the percentage of literacy 10.09 per cent, 10.41 per cent and 10.13 per cent respectively. In this way if we see the other censuses than we will find almost same pace of progress.

Another very low literacy having district is Bardhwan, where 26.89 per cent scheduled caste people are living with its total population. Scheduled castes of this district are also not very conscious regarding their education, which is observed from their literacy performance. Their literacy rate is recorded in the census 2011 is only 61.19 per cent which is lower than the state level scheduled caste literacy performance. Their literacy position in the state is twelfth. It is observed from the all census of the state the district has very poor record of performance in education by the scheduled caste people. In the same way if we see the scheduled caste participation in education in the district Birbhum, than it is found that this district also carries very bad message to the Nation regarding their education. But this district possesses good number of scheduled caste people. According to the census 2001 of the state it is found that 29.53 per cent scheduled caste people are living in the district. Whereas their participation level of scheduled caste people in education is too lower than state level as well as Nation level of participation of scheduled caste in education. According to 1961 census of the district SCs literacy rate was recorded only 7.32 per cent and in 2011 census their percentage of literacy is recorded only 54.94 per cent.

District wise participation of scheduled caste in education in West Bengal or development of education among scheduled caste may be better understood from their decadal growth rate of literacy. As it is found from the above description that all the districts of the state are not equally progressive in education and their rate of growth also varies from district to district. In the following table decadal growth rate of scheduled caste people in different districts are shown below.

Table 5.4: Decadal Growth of Education among Scheduled Castes in a Districts of West Bengal from 1961-2001

Sl. No.	*State/Districts*	*1961-1971*	*1971-1981*	*1981-1991*	*1991-2001*
1.	West Bengal	4.22	6.62	17.79	16.83
2.	Koch Bihar	1.1	6.93	15.86	25.23
3.	Jalpaiguri	7.09	6.19	18.29	20.53
4.	Darjeeling	2.47	7.06	14.53	16.13
5.	Uttar Dinajpur	5.07	4.12	13.02	17.01
6.	Daxin Dinajpur	–	–	–	–
7.	Maldah	2.98	6.92	13.48	17.28
8.	Murshidabad	2.66	5.6	15.72	16.12
9.	Nadia	4.51	6.24	17.81	17.77
10.	North 24 Paragana	7.07	7.2	20.23	17.28
11.	South 24 Paragana	–	–	–	9.22
12.	Kolkata	3.57	10.95	13.94	14.01
13.	Haora	9.45	3.13	16.07	16.26
14.	Hugli	1.41	9.29	18.16	15.44
15.	Medinipur	4.6	7.26	27.8	9.01
16.	Bankura	3.21	4.84	15.03	12.96
17.	Puruliya	3.36	8.05	13.35	13.34
18.	Burdhwan	1.58	4.44	20.78	15.42
19.	Birbhum	2.81	4.66	12.87	18.08

The above table reveals that decadal growth rate of scheduled caste literacy of the state is 4.22 during 1961-1971, 6.62 in 1971-1981, 17.79 in 1981-1991 and 16.83 in 1991-2001 decade. The highest decadal growth rate is recorded in the district Koch Bihar which is 25.23 during 1991-2001, followed by the district Jalpariguri 20.53, Birbhum 18.08 and Nadia 17.77. The district Maldah and North 24 Paragana has the same decadal growth rate of scheduled caste education during 1991-2001. The district Uttar Dinajpur and Daxin Dinajpur was a single district before 1991 census of the state. So, the decadal growth rate of scheduled caste education shown before 1991 census is for the both district. All other districts of the state could not achieve the state level growth rate of scheduled caste education during 1991-2001. Though few of these district literacy rate of scheduled caste is better than the state level SCs literacy rate, still their decadal growth rate is lower than the state level growth rate. But it would be wise to mention here that decadal growth rate of scheduled caste participation in education of all districts are gradually increasing day-by-day.

DEVELOPMENT OF EDUCATION AMONG VARIOUS COMMUNITY GROUPS OF SCHEDULED CASTE IN THE STATE

In the state West Bengal as we have found that, there are fifty nine (59) sub-communities among the scheduled caste people. Out of these fifty nine only very few groups are very successful in the field of education and majority of scheduled castes groups remain unsuccessful. There are some communities of SCs groups concentrated in the urban areas, they are educationally advanced than the others. Besides, there are some communities their socio-economical condition is good in comparison to the others groups of the scheduled caste of the state, they could progress in all sides including education. It is reported from the table that some of the scheduled caste people are gradually progressing in the field of education, as it is found from the various census report of the state. Again the growth rate of education in decadal wise if someone observe than it would be found that decadal growth rate of each community of the scheduled caste in the state is different from each other. There are some very strong scheduled caste group from the very past, their participation in education also remarkable, even their literacy rate is found far better than so called general people of the state. In the following Table 5.5/ paragraph development of education in each scheduled caste community in various censuses report in shown.

The table shows that out of fifty nine (59) sub-communities twenty seven (27) sub-communities are cross the measuring line of the literacy. The scheduled caste literacy rate in West Bengal is 68.24 per cent, this limit crossed by the following community groups. They are—Sunri, Sarki, Bahelia, Baiti, Damai, Dhoba, Doai, Doshad, Halakhor, jalia Kaibarta, Jhalo Malo, Kadar, Kanjar, Kandra, Khatik, Konwar, Kotal, lalbegi, Namasudra, Nat, Pan, Pasi, Rajbanshi, Patni, Pod and Tiyr; and rest of the 32 scheduled caste community groups lies below of the measuring line of the state. Again if we analyze their development of education each community wise than we find that—

Bagdi, Duley is the scheduled caste group of the state, size wise their position is third highest in the state according to the census 2001. But in case of education their position is very bad in comparison to the development of education among scheduled caste. It is recorded from the above table that in 1961 literacy rate of this group was recorded only 8.74 per cent whereas, literacy of scheduled caste in the state was recorded 13.58 per cent, again, in 1971 their percentage was 10.79 per cent and state level percentage was 17.80 per cent, in 1981 13.96 per cent and

Table 5.5: Distribution of Literacy Rate among Different Communities of Scheduled Castes in West Bengal in 1961-2011

Sl. No.	*State/Districts*	*1961*	*1971*	*1981*	*1991*	*2001*	**2011*
1.	All Scheduled Castes	13.58	17.80	24.42	42.21	59.04	68.26
2.	Bagdi, Duley	8.74	10.79	13.96	30.02	47.72	56.92
3.	Bahelia	11.56	14.39	22.53	39.21	59.61	68.81
4.	Baiti	12.72	17.99	32.92	51.93	68.84	78.04
5.	Bantar	15.40	18.05	17.73	35.19	33.11	42.31
6.	Bauri	5.47	10.11	9.42	21.47	37.46	46.66
7.	Beldar	9.64	20.21	18.70	31.91	39.79	48.99
8.	Bhoğta	3.14	33.33	18.03	35.91	47.89	57.09
9.	Bhuimali	11.32	17.41	21.22	39.63	57.13	66.33
10.	Bhuiya	7.07	9.95	14.22	33.84	42.09	51.29
11.	Bind	6.57	10.86	12.70	20.76	35.01	44.21
12.	Chamar, Charmakar, Mochi, Muchi, Rabidas, Ruidas, Rishi	8.34	12.00	14.42	28.08	46.99	56.19
13.	Chaupal	3.25	16.34	20.76	28.52	43.15	52.35
14.	Dabgar	29.17	20.43	22.39	52.84	34.51	43.71
15.	Damai (Nepali)	21.07	37.25	37.46	52.44	69.83	79.03
16.	Dhoba, Dhobi	18.92	24.28	38.79	62.07	73.87	83.07
17.	Doai	6.23	17.32	22.55	47.11	60.09	69.29
18.	Dom, Dhangad	7.06	9.88	12.58	29.09	46.02	55.22
19.	Dosadh, Dusadh, Dhari, Dharhi	12.92	16.67	23.67	44.23	59.56	68.76
20.	Ghasi	5.82	10.19	9.01	26.55	30.45	39.65
21.	Gonrhi	5.64	18.61	25.21	37.87	56.04	65.24
22.	Halalkhor	24.54	10.43	29.90	51.47	68.69	77.89
23.	Hari, Mehtar, Mehtor, Bhangi	7.69	10.77	15.28	42.10	49.45	58.65
24.	Jalia Kaibartta	17.95	20.47	30.16	49.31	64.85	74.05
25.	Jhalo Malo, Malo	14.50	19.18	25.51	42.52	60.33	69.53
26.	Kadar	12.16	22.81	25.50	30.75	69.74	78.94
27.	Kami (Nepali)	18.05	27.91	34.70	49.45	68.78	77.98
28.	Kandra	15.11	24.02	31.49	60.09	72.15	81.35
29.	Kanjar	16.16	8.18	16.03	32.45	65.35	74.55
30.	Kaora	9.65	17.30	17.81	32.32	52.99	62.19
31.	Karenga, Koranga	9.48	12.33	18.39	35.68	54.81	64.01
32.	Kaur	12.33	14.47	16.46	38.72	52.14	61.34
33.	Keot, Keyot	13.81	16.57	23.21	41.75	53.79	62.99
34.	Khaira	5.33	9.17	10.98	24.20	42.28	51.48
35.	Khatik	25.33	17.96	30.01	42.11	68.94	78.14
36.	Koch	8.57	16.13	15.19	28.71	42.96	52.16
37.	Konai	7.40	9.06	15.91	30.57	49.65	58.85
38.	Konwar	15.66	24.50	45.69	58.37	82.95	92.15
39.	Kotal	12.48	14.44	21.75	45.35	59.69	68.89
40.	Kurariar	5.40	21.95	25.14	42.20	56.72	65.92
41.	Lalbegi	18.11	21.53	25.87	51.82	67.15	76.35
42.	Lohar	8.30	12.37	15.09	29.73	46.50	55.70
43.	Mahar	11.79	13.35	19.85	40.26	52.60	61.80
44.	Mal	5.91	9.58	12.16	26.56	39.63	48.83

(Contd.)

Sl. No.	State/Districts	1961	1971	1981	1991	2001	*2011
45.	Mallah	14.06	15.41	23.80	37.65	53.86	63.06
46.	Musahar	3.16	8.28	5.30	15.75	15.25	24.45
47.	Namasudra	21.03	26.86	35.87	56.18	71.93	81.13
48.	Nat	4.45	39.19	31.25	49.67	59.25	68.45
49.	Nuniya	11.02	15.85	20.75	39.39	54.19	63.39
50.	Paliya	11.63	20.88	18.46	30.96	41.84	51.04
51.	Pan, Sawasi	16.91	16.37	27.25	54.91	61.00	70.20
52.	Pasi	15.61	7.89	26.79	46.32	64.11	73.31
53.	Patni	16.19	18.93	25.44	49.40	64.49	73.69
54.	Pod, Poundra	21.68	27.31	36.49	56.05	72.10	81.30
55.	Rajbanshi	14.75	17.56	24.65	40.71	60.14	69.34
56.	Rajwar	9.17	11.36	16.63	38.68	46.41	55.61
57.	Sarki (Nepali)	14.35	26.02	27.32	49.30	62.48	71.68
58.	Sunri (Excluding Saha	28.58	22.41	54.95	65.96	82.28	91.48
59.	Tiyar	8.06	20.40	25.33	45.16	62.11	71.31
60.	Turi	7.48	12.95	14.25	27.62	40.59	49.79
61.	Unclassified	15.01	20.20	-	37.39	62.19	71.39

*Projected data.
Source: Census reports of India, RGI 1961-2001.

state level 24.42 per cent, in 1991 30.02 per cent and state level performance was 42.21 per cent and in 2001 census participation rate in education by this group was recorded 47.72 per cent, but all scheduled caste participation rate was recorded 59.04 per cent which too high than this group. And finally in the latest census i.e. 2011 their literacy rate is recorded as only 56.92 per cent. So, it is reveals that this group of scheduled caste in the state requires more attention from the state government to bring them in to the light of education.

Participation in education of Bahelia a group of scheduled caste is recorded above the state level scheduled caste participation in education in 2011 census of the state. It is found that this is the marginal group of the state among the scheduled caste. But in case of their education they are marginal in their position. Initially their participation level in education was less than the measuring line of the state. Their percentage of literacy was recorded in the census 1961 is 11.56 per cent, in 1971 14.39 per cent, in 1981 22.53 per cent and 1991 39.21 per cent, all these record was below than the measuring line of the state. But it is only 2001and 2011 census where their literacy is found above than the measuring line which is 59.61 per cent and 68.81 per cent respectively.

Another educationally very strong scheduled caste community in the state is Baiti. Their population percentage in the state is only 0.02 per cent but their literacy percentage is 78.04 per cent according to the census 2011. It is found from the table that in 1961 their percentage in educational literacy was less than the state level scheduled caste people, but after that period their participation level in education was increased rapidly and within a very short period they could remain above the state level of position. It is found from the table that development of education was very of this group people during 1981 to 1991 i.e. in 1981 their literacy percentage was 32.92 per cent and immediately their percentage in education was increased up to 51.93 per cent it means growth rate of education of the group is 19.01 per cent.

Banter is one of the sub-castes of the scheduled caste group in the state; their population percentage is only 0.06 per cent. But the above table reveals that this is one of the peculiar groups of scheduled caste whose development in education is decreasing day by day. The table reported that in 1961 census their literacy percentage was recorded 15.40 per cent which was above than the state level scheduled caste literacy percentage, again in 1971 census their literacy rate was recorded 18.05 per cent which was also better than the state's measuring level. But after that census literacy percentage of this group of scheduled caste was decreased, which was reported that in 1981 17.73 per cent, in 1991 census their percentage again increased up to 35.19 per cent and in 2001 again decreased up to 33.11 per cent and finally in 2011 their performance increased upto 42.31 per cent. So, it is found that the growth of education of this group of people is not static.

According to the above table it may be mentioned that other group like—Bauri, Beldar, Bhogta, Bhuiya, Bind, Chamar or Charmakar or Rabidas, Chaupal these scheduled castes people also backward in their educational field. It is reported by the above table that all the mentioned scheduled caste people's participation in education is lower than the measuring level of the state. It is found from the report that literacy percentage is recorded according to the census 2011, Bauri 46.66 per cent, Beldar 48.99 per cent, Bhogta 57.09 per cent, Bhuimali is another group which is some extent better than the others which is 66.33 per cent, Bhuiya 51.29 per cent, Bind 44.21 per cent, and Chamar or Charmakar 56.19 per cent, Chaupal 52.35 per cent literacy rate. From this literacy rate it can be observed that what is their participation in education and how conscious they are regarding their education? It is not that their literacy rate is lower in 2011 census report, but it is observed in all the census reports of the state that their educational participation is very poor in comparison to the other sub caste of scheduled caste community.

Dabgar is another marginal group of scheduled caste in West Bengal whose population percentage in the state is too low. Though their number is very low but they were very much conscious regarding their education so far their literacy rate shown in various census of the state is concerned. Their literacy rate is found 29.17 per cent in 1961, 20.43 per cent in 1971, and 52.84 per cent in 1991 census of the state which is above than the measuring line of the state. But on the other hand their performance is found low than the measuring line of the state in the year 1981, which recorded only 20.76 per cent, in 2001 34.51 per cent and in 2011 43.71 per cent which is decrease percentage than the previous year census. It reveals that they are conscious enough regarding their education but, may be due to certain reason their percentage in education have been decrease in the recent census of the state.

The scheduled caste people like Damai (Nepali), Dhoba or Dhobi, Doai, Dom or Dhangad, Dosadh or Dhari are educationally developed group in the state except Dom. All the mentioned groups are found better participative in education in all the census of the state. The census reports reveals that Damai is a Nepali scheduled caste community whose literacy percentage is recorded in 2011 is 79.03 per cent it is also reveals that all the previous record like in 1961 21.07 per cent, in 1971 37.25 per cent, in 1981 37.46 per cent in 1991 52.44 per cent and 2001 census 69.83 per cent, of literacy rates are above than the measuring level of the state. In the same way Dhoba or Dhobi is another very strong group in the field of education in the state. As it is found from the various sources that this group of scheduled caste people are basically living in the urban areas, as their occupation required. So, they get urban areas or environment to nurture their children and as a result their participation in education gets increase day by day. According to the census 2011 their percentage of literacy recorded 83.07 per cent which is too higher than the measuring level of the state literacy of scheduled caste. If we see the development of education of previous censuses than it is found that in all the census years their participation in education is found high such as—in 1961 their percentage of literacy was 18.92 per cent, in 1971 24.28 per cent, in 1981 38.79 per cent in 1991 62.07 per cent and in 2001 is 73.87 per cent. On the other hand Doai and Dosadh also found having good participation in education. It would be better to mention here is that these two groups had no good records in education up to 1981 census. But later on they could improve their participation level in education by increasing their literacy percentage in the state. But Dom another group of scheduled caste whose participation in education is found poor in comparison to the other group of scheduled caste. Their education percentage is recorded in 2011 is only 55.22 per cent, and their previous record also found very poor in comparison to the other scheduled caste group of the state.

Another educationally backward group of scheduled castes are Ghasi, Gonrhi and Hari or Mehtor as revealed by the above mentioned table. Their participation in education is found very poor in comparison to the other group of scheduled caste in the state. Out of these group of SCs, very low literacy rate is found among Ghasi, whose percentage of literacy is recorded in the census 2011 is only 39.65 per cent which is very low than the measuring level of the SCs literacy of the state. In the same way literacy rate of the group Gonrhi and Hari is recorded only 65.24 per cent and 58.65 per cent in 2001 respectively. Their literacy rate was recorded very low such as Ghasi 5.82 per cent, Gonrhi 5.64 per cent and 7.69 per cent among Hari or Bhangi in 1961 census.

The above table also reveals that scheduled caste group like Halakhor, Jalia Kaibarta, Jhalo-Malo, Kadar, Kami, Kandra and Kanjar are having good academic record in various census of the state. Out of these scheduled caste group Kandra possess the highest position in the rank of literacy progress. Their literacy percentage is 81.35 per cent according to the census 2011; they had good record in the previous censuses of the state. The another sub caste Kadar literacy rate is 78.94 per cent, Kami (Nepali) 77.98 per cent, Kanjar 74.55 per cent, Jalia Kaibarta 74.05 per cent and Jhalo Malo or Jhalo 69.53 per cent according to the census 2011 shown in the above table. If we see the growth rate of these groups of scheduled caste, than it is found that their growth rate is also varies from census to census. In 1961 literacy rate Jalia Kaibarta was 17.95 per cent and in the next census it increases up to only 20.47 per cent i.e. growth rate is here only 2.52 per cent, but in the next census i.e. in 1981 it increase up to 30.16 per cent from 20.47 per cent; the growth rate in this census is 9.69 per cent. Again in the next census their percentage of education increased up to 49.31 per cent. So, it is found that Jalia Kaibarta group of SCs are increasing their number of participation in education in the state. In the same way Jhalo Malo is also increased their number of participation in education in every census in a certain growth rate. In 1961 census their participation level of education was 14.50 per cent and in 1971 they increase their literacy rate up to 19.18 per cent only, after in 1981 their percentage stood up to 25.51 per cent and in 1991 30.75 per cent. It is seen that their literacy percentage was became lower in 1991 suddenly, but in 2001 census they could recover their position by showing literacy rate up to 60.33 per cent. Kadar another group of scheduled caste community could show their education position is higher than many other group of scheduled caste in the state. The above table reported that in the census 1961 their participation in education was lower than the state level SCs literacy rate, but in the census 1971 and 1981 their position in education was higher than the state level scheduled caste literacy rate. Again their position went below than the state level growth in 1991 census which was only 30.75 per cent, but again in the next census they could progress a lot in the field of education. It shows that this group of scheduled caste community is very much concerned about their education. In the same way we find the progress of education among Kami (Nepali) and Kandra group of SCs. They are also conscious enough regarding their education which is reveal from their literacy percentage shown in the various censuses of the state reported in the above table. Kanjar are very marginal number in their population position. But they are very much conscious enough regarding their education. Initially they could not show their position in the field of education, but in the 2001 census their position remained above than the all SCs literacy of the state.

The table also reveals that low literate people are found among the scheduled caste group like—Kaora 62.19 per cent, Karenga or Koranga 64.01 per cent, Kaur 61.34 per cent, Keot 62.99 per cent, Khaira 51.48 per cent, Koch 52.16 per cent, Konai 58.85 per cent, Kurariar 65.92 per cent, Lohar 55.70 per cent, Mahar 61.80 per cent, Mal 48.83 per cent, Mallah 63.06 per cent, Musahar 24.45 per cent, Nunniya 63.39 per cent, Paliya 51.04 per cent, Rajwar 55.61 per cent and Turi 49.79 per cent literacy rate according to the census 2011 report of the state. It would be worthwhile to mention here that these scheduled castes are not only backward in education rather they are backward in all aspect of their life.

On the other hand the table also reveals that scheduled caste group having good literacy percentage such as—Khatik 78.14 per cent, Konowar 92.15 per cent, Kotal 68.89 per cent, Lalbegi 76.35 per cent, Namasudra 81.13 per cent, Nat 68.45 per cent, Pan or Sawasi 70.20 per cent, Pasi 73.31 per cent, Patni 73.69 per cent, Pod or Poundra 81.30 per cent, Rajbanshi 69.34 per cent, Sarki (Nepali) 71.68 per cent, Sunri (Excluding Saha) 91.48 per cent, Tiyar 71.31 per cent and unclassified group of scheduled caste literacy rate is recorded according to the census 2011 in the state. Out of these groups of SCs highest literacy rate is found among Konowar with 92.15 per cent, may be this is the group whose literacy percentage is highest among the scheduled caste group. Another very strong literate group is Sunri with literacy 91.48 per cent followed by Pod and Namasudra community. All the above mentioned groups are developed almost in all sides of their life. Rajbanshi and Namasudra community are second highest and third highest scheduled caste group in the state so far their number of population is concerned.

So, from the above table it is found that highest educated group is Konowar with 92.15 per cent and lowest educated group is Musahar with only 24.45 per cent of literacy among the scheduled caste of the state. This group of scheduled caste needs more attention and care from the government to make them conscious about the education to bring them into the state level of literacy of the state.

DEVELOPMENT OF NAMASUDRA IN EDUCATION IN WEST BENGAL

The Namasudras are very strong scheduled caste group in West Bengal. They stood second position in the scheduled caste population of West Bengal; they share 17.40 per cent to the total scheduled caste of the state according to the census 2001 of West Bengal. Namasudras are the indigenous group of the state. As it is mentioned earlier that Namasudras in West Bengal are very strong among the scheduled caste of the state; so they are very sound in education in comparison to the other group of scheduled caste in the state. In the Table 5.6 literacy percentages of Namasudra people are shown from 1961-2011 census of West Bengal.

Table 5.6: Literacy of Namasudra and Scheduled Caste People

Sl. No.	*West Bengal*	*1961*	*1971*	*1981*	*1991*	*2001*	*2011**
1.	Scheduled Castes	13.58	17.80	24.42	42.21	59.04	68.26
2.	Namasudra	21.03	26.86	35.87	56.18	71.93	81.13

*Projected data 2011.

Source: Census reports of India, RGI, 1961-2001.

The Namasudra people in West Bengal are to some extent developed in the field of education in comparison to the other community group among scheduled caste of the state. Their present literacy rate is 81.13 per cent according to the census 2011. In the census 1961 of West Bengal their literacy rate was 21.03 per cent, 26.86 per cent in 1971, 35.87 per cent in 1981, 56.18 per cent in 1991 and 71.93 per cent in 2001. The present literacy rate of the group is higher than the state level scheduled castes literacy rate. It is also reveal from the table above that the literacy rate of the Namasudra people is higher than the all census report in West Bengal, 1961, 1971, 1981, 1991, 2001 and 2011. This progress in the field of education reveals that the Namasudra people in West Bengal are very conscious about their rights, duties and responsibilities towards their life, society and to the country as well.

It is also reveals from the above table that in each census the literacy rate of scheduled caste remains below than the Namasudras in the state. According to the census 1961 the literacy rate of SCs was 13.58 per cent, whereas Namasudra people literacy rate was 21.03 per cent. Again in 1971 the SCs literacy rate was 17.80 per cent and Namasudra people literacy was 26.86 per cent. In 1981 the participation of SCs in education was 24.42 per cent and Namasudra people literacy was 35.87 per cent. In this year the difference literacy rate was observed 11.45, but in 1991 this difference increased up to 13.97. In this year literacy among all scheduled caste was found 42.21 per cent, but Namasudra literacy was observed 56.18 per cent. It reveals that growth rate of Namasudras in education is better than all scheduled caste literacy growth.

Finally, in 2011 census of the state Namasudra literacy is recorded maximum of 81.13 per cent and all scheduled caste literacy rate is observed 68.24 per cent. So, it is found from the above table that trend of development of Namasudras in education is very good in the state.

Namasudras in West Bengal are not only sound in education, but they are very sound in their economics and political fields also. In this regard it may be mentioned that Das, B. (1986) expressed that in Bengal during the period of King Gopal and other Kings of his dynasty and Raja Sitaram they were economically sound. They belonged to the Aristocratic community in culture and dignity and magnitude of their livelihood was high. But due to political changes and violence of untouchablity incited during the reign of Raja Ballov Sen Namasudras people were forced to accept the inhuman rules. But the Namasudras opposed to accept the inhuman rules. The King with all powers operated his force against them and drove them away from their ancestral land tortured mercilessly and announced all over his state that Namasudras are 'Chandals', 'Charal' and untouchables. Thus they were placed in the lowest class of the Hindu society. So, from that time onward though they were considered lower caste of the society and migrated to different places of India, but they could maintain their life style above than any other sub-caste of scheduled caste group. Consequently, they are able to progress in every sphere of their life in the society all over the country. Comparative statement of participation of Namasudras and scheduled caste in education may be expressed through the histogram (Fig. 5.3), which is shown below.

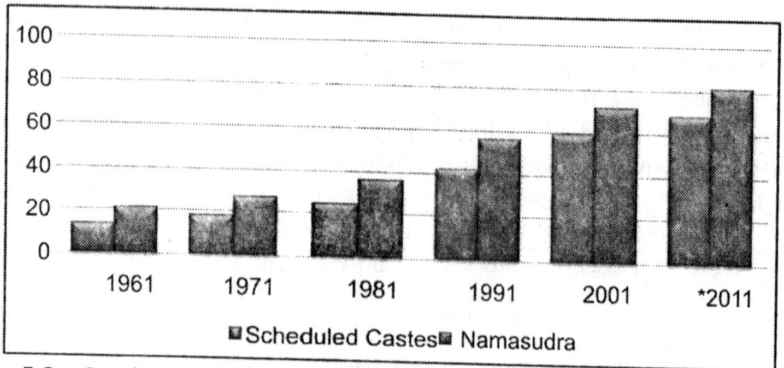

Fig. 5.3: Graphical Representation of Literacy Among Scheduled Caste and Namasudras in Various Years of West Bengal

It is found from the above graph that how literacy growth among Namasudras are remain above than all the scheduled caste literacy growth in every year of the state. It is also observed from the above graph that growth rate of both i.e. Namasudras and Scheduled caste is almost same.

Table 5.7: Decadal wise Growth of Namasudra and Scheduled Caste People in Education

Sl. No.	*West Bengal*	*1961-1971*	*1971-1981*	*1981-1991*	*1991-2001*
1.	Scheduled Castes	4.22	6.62	17.79	16.83
2.	Namasudra	5.83	9.01	20.31	15.75

Source: Calculated based on various census reports.

The above mentioned Table 5.7 reveals the decadal growth of education among Namasudra and scheduled caste of West Bengal in various censuses. It is seen from the table that growth rate of Namasudra literacy in West Bengal in the early censuses was very fast, but later on it came down. It is found from the table that decadal variation of growth rate among Namasudra people in the state was 5.83 per cent in 1961-1971, whereas all scheduled caste rate was only 4.22 per cent in the same year. In the same way 9.01 per cent among Namasudra and 6.62 per cent among all scheduled caste is found in the year 1971-1981, 20.31 per cent among Namasudra and 17.79 per cent among scheduled caste in 1981-1991. It also reveals that growth rate of Namasudra people in education always remain above than the state level scheduled caste literacy growth so far the above table is concerned. But suddenly in the decade 1991-2001 growth rate of Namasudra all scheduled caste people in education was came down. It is seen from the above table that in this decade Namasudra people growth rate came down into 15.75 per cent and all scheduled caste people growth rate came down into 16.83 per cent. Decadal growth of education of Namasudras and Scheduled caste may be clearly expressed through a polygon. A polygon is prepared and shown below:

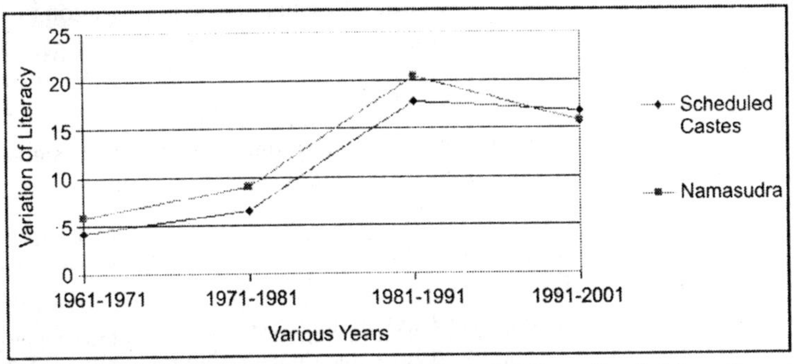

Fig. 5.4: Graphical Representation of Decadal Growth of Education of Namasudras and Scheduled Caste

Table 5.8: District wise Literacy Rate of Namasudra and Scheduled Caste People in West Bengal in 2001

Sl. No.	*Name of the Districts*	*2001*		**2011*	
		Namasudra	*SC*	*Namasudra*	*SC*
1.	West Bengal	71.93	59.04	81.13	68.26
2.	Darjiling	61.34	62.43	70.54	71.63
3.	Jalpaiguri	57.01	61.87	66.21	81.07
4.	Kochbihar	53.19	66.30	62.39	75.50
5.	South Dinaspur	53.09	54.55	62.29	63.75
6.	Hugli	68.08	56.10	77.28	65.30
7.	Kolkata	73.19	70.54	82.39	79.74
8.	Malda	55.87	51.17	65.07	60.37
9.	Midnapur	67.27	63.57	76.47	72.77
10.	Nadia	61.81	63.09	71.01	72.29
11.	South 24 Paragana	65.65	59.01	74.85	68.21
12.	North 24 Paragana	69.35	70.79	78.85	79.99
13.	Uttar Dinajpur	54.62	50.06	63.82	59.26
14.	Burdwan	64.19	51.99	73.39	61.19
15.	Birbhum	66.54	45.74	75.74	54.94
16.	Bankura	62.44	42.92	71.64	52.12
17.	Howrah	67.10	61.13	76.30	70.33
18.	Murshidabad	61.16	48.91	70.36	58.11
19.	Puruliya	85.40	45.15	94.60	54.35

The above polygon expresses decadal growth trends of Namasudras and Scheduled caste people in education of the state West Bengal.

As it is mentioned above that Namasudra people are found all the districts of West Bengal; but their academic developments are not equal in all the districts.

The above Table 5.8 expresses that the district wise participation of Namasudra people as well as scheduled castes people in education in the census 2001 and 2011. In the table highest literacy i.e. above 80 per cent among the Namasudra people found in the districts are Puruliya 94.60 per cent whereas scheduled caste literacy percentage of the district is only 54.35 per cent, than 82.39 per cent among Namasudra in Kolkata and 79.74 per cent among scheduled caste. The districts having more than 70 per cent literacy of Namasudra people are North 24 Paragana 78.55 per cent, Midnapur 76.47 per cent, Birbhum 75.74 per cent, Howrah 76.30 per cent and Hugli 77.28 per cent, Darjiling 70.54 per cent, Nadia 71.01 per cent, Burdwan 73.39 per cent, Bankura, 71.64 per cent and Murshidabad 70.36 per cent. Again the districts having below 65 per cent are Uttar Dinajpur 63.82 per cent, Jalpaiguri, 66.21 per cent, Koochbihar 62.39 per cent and Daxin Dinajpur 62.29 per cent.

The above table also reveals that almost all the districts having higher literacy of Namasudra in education in comparison to the state level scheduled caste literacy percentage. But it is only four districts of the state having higher literacy among scheduled caste in comparison to the Namasudra people. The districts are North 24 Paragana 79.99 per cent of scheduled caste, whereas Namasudra people's literacy is 78.55 per cent, than Koochbihar 75.50 per cent among scheduled caste and 62.39 per cent among Namasudras, Jalpaiguri 71.07 per cent, and 66.21 per cent and in Darjiling 71.63 per cent among scheduled caste and 70.54 per cent among Namasudras.

The table above again explains that Namasudras in West Bengal are comparatively stronger in the field of education in comparison to the few scheduled caste group as well as all scheduled caste people. As it is found from the history that Namasudra in Bengal were very strong group, so they could keep their developmental trend in the present time social system also. Actually though they have been recognized as the scheduled caste or lower group people in the society, but they keep themselves above in every aspects than the scheduled caste in the West Bengal society. But in some cases, still they are living at the lowest level social structure due to their low socio economic condition and due to the social system imposed over them by the so called higher caste people in the society. The people of this group living under that sector are still can't able to get even minimum facilities required by them.

However, majority of this group of people are living in rural areas of the state, and maximum of them are still dependent on agriculture and daily wages. During the field visit of the researcher, it is found in some cases that there are some family in the district Nadia and North 24 Paragana, they are to think regularly about their food; and in that situation their reply was that in such situation they can't think of sending their children to the school, though govt. has introduced free and compulsory education to the all people irrespective of caste, creed, community, sex, race and languages. Because of these mentioned reasons some of the districts of West Bengal still could not show the education level high of the scheduled caste and Namasudras. But there are some districts which are developed in many sides; consequently they could show their education level in very high position. But development of a state does not mean to develop one group or few group in some fields, development means progress of all people in all sides.

VI

Problems, Prospects and Suggestions

The scheduled caste are facing lot of problems in their day-to-day life such as–ethnic/racial problems, social problems, cultural problems, economic problem and also problem in education. The situation of scheduled castes in West Bengal is not an exception. The intra community disparities are also visible among the scheduled caste.

Namasudra students of West Bengal faces a number of problems in their education process; as a result their participation level in education is found lower than many other groups of people living in the state. The problems which commonly faced by the Namasudra students in West Bengal are broadly categorized as—*Home related problem, school related problem, teacher related problem, reading related problem and problem in general.*

ANALYSIS OF HOME RELATED PROBLEM

Under home related problems various type of problems have been specified and data has been collected. Data has been collected from N-300 students of West Bengal. Analysis of the data collected through the tools from respondents have been shown in Table 6.1.

Table 6.1: Father's Occupation

States	Agriculture	Business	Govt. Service	Private Sector	Labourer	Others
West Bengal	50 (16.66%)	72 (24%)	16 (5.33%)	8 (2.66%)	74 (24.66%)	80 (26.66%)

The Table 6.1 reveals only 16.66 per cent people are cultivator in West Bengal. It is also reveals from the above table that only 24 per cent parent of Namasudra people are businessman, in West Bengal. It is found that more people in West Bengal are engaged in business. Again it is found from the table that only 5.33 per cent people are doing government service in West Bengal. Again, 2.66 per cent Namasudra people are working in private sector in West Bengal. The report reveals that the labour class people are found more in West Bengal, which is 24.66 per cent. The Namasudra parent whose children go to school in West Bengal, they are mostly engaged in works which is 26.66 per cent.

Table 6.2: Problems related to Home

Nature of the Problems	*Yes*	*No*
Parents encourage in study	300 (100%)	0
Remain absent in school for domestic works	33 (11%)	267 (89%)
Separate accommodation at your home for reading	158 (52.66%)	142 (47.33%)
Arrangement of chair, table etc. at home for study	144 (48%)	156 (52%)
Family bear necessary expenditure for study	156 (52%)	144 (48%)

The table reveals that regarding the encouragement received from parent by the Namasudra people it is found in West Bengal that all the students i.e. 100 per cent students reading secondary stage get encouragement from their parents in their study at their home. This actually reveals that how the people of West Bengal are progressive in education. They took all the troubles for their children education though they are socio-economically very poor in comparison to the other groups of people in the state. It is revealed from the above table that in West Bengal 11 per cent students agree that they remain absent in the school due to their domestic work, and rest of the 89 per cent student do not agree in this or they do not find any problem regarding this. It is very necessary to have separate accommodation for study at home. Because it creates interest as well as arouse motivation in the students mind for study. If the students do not get good accommodation facilities to study in their home than definitely they will show very less interest in their study and which will create problem of absent in the school, stagnation in the class and drop out problem in the school. In West Bengal 47.33 per cent of students do not have their separate accommodation at their home for reading; but 52.66 per cent students of West Bengal said that they have separate accommodation for reading. So, it is found that a good number of students from both the state do not have any separate accommodation at their home for reading. Now, it may be imaginable that without having reading facilities what can be expected from them.

The above table again reveals that 48 per cent of students in West Bengal replied that they have necessary arrangement for reading such as—chair, table and other things related to it; but majority of the students i.e. 52 per cent of Namasudra students are not having necessary arrangement of study such as—chair, table and others things.

Again it is observed from the above table that 52 per cent of Namasudra students replied that they have no money problem, because their family can bear their expenditure necessary for their study purpose. But 48 per cent of Namasudra students responded that their family cannot bear their expenditure necessary for their study.

PROBLEMS RELATED TO SCHOOL

Namasudra students of and West Bengal have some school related problems which are directly related to the school itself. Because of those problems these groups of people are unable to continue their study for long time in their life. These problems related to school may be represented in the following ways and data has been collected accordingly.

Problem of School Distance: The Table 6.3 reveals that in West Bengal it is found that 44.33 per cent of Namasudra students revealed that their school is ½ km far from their home, 21 per cent of students are scattered within 1 km around the school, 25.33 per cent of students expressed that their school is 2 km away from their home and only 9.33 per cent of students said that their school is 3 km or more km from their home.

Table 6.3: Distance of School from the Home of Namasudra Students

States	*About ½ km*	*About 1 km*	*About 2 km*	*3 km or more*
West Bengal	133 (44.33%)	63 (21%)	76 (25.33%)	28 (9.33%)

Table 6.4: Communication Used by the Namasudra Students

States	*On foot*	*By bicycle*	*By Bus*	*By own car*
West Bengal	208 (69.33%)	87 (29%)	5 (1.66%)	0

The above Table 6.4 shows that 69.33 per cent of Namasudra students goes to school on foot, 29 per cent students by bicycle and only 1.66 per cent of students go to school by bus, but by own car nobody goes to school in the state. In West Bengal School are situated within very short distance, so their student has to face less communication.

Problems of Within School Faced by Namasudra Students in West Bengal: Namasudra students of West Bengal also face some school problems which are within school. In the school they come across some problems in various ways in various forms. The nature of problems and respondents percentage is shown in Table 6.5.

Table 6.5: Problem related to School

Nature of the problems	*Yes*	*No*
Sitting comfortably in the class room	290 (96.66%)	10 (3.33%)
Mixing up with other students of the school	294 (98%)	6 (2%)
Participating in other affairs of school beside study	255 (85%)	45 (15%)
Paying all subscriptions exam. Fees etc. in due time	189 (63%)	111 (37%)

From the above table it is observed that in West Bengal 96.66 per cent of Namasudra students said that they have sufficient sitting arrangement and they can sit comfortably in their class, and only 3.33 per cent of them have complaint that they cannot sit comfortably in their class. It shows that though the least number of students complaint against the comfortable sitting in the class, but that problem still exist in the class due to which some students may not be interested to go school regularly. But the problem of mixing up with the other students is existed more among the Namasudra people in school in the state West Bengal. It reveals from the statement that in West Bengal still caste system problem is prevailing in the society, and due to which some people hesitate to mix up with the other caste so called general caste people in any situation. There are some problems such as inferiority, inefficiency, lack of encouragement, mental support and problem with family background due to which some students hesitate to take part to any school affairs in addition to their study. Keeping in mind all these point the researcher has collected data to see their accessibility of participation in school affairs in addition to their study. Data collected through the questionnaire revealed that in West Bengal 85 per cent of Namasudra students can take part in other affairs of school in addition to their study, and 15 per cent of students do not able to take part in any school affairs in addition to their study; may be due the above mentioned reasons.

So far the economic condition is concerned, Namasudra people living in very poor condition in the state. Due to this reason only large number of Namasudra people are still backward in all aspect. Education is closely related to the economic condition of the people. From the above table it is found that 63 per cent of students can pay their necessary fees to the school in due time in West Bengal, and 37 per cent of students are not able to pay their fees to the school in due time. So far the report is concerned the economic condition of West Bengal Namasudra students is very pathetic in this regard.

Table 6.6: Problem related to Garments/Books/Library/School Time

Nature of Problems	*Yes*	*No*
Book or economic help from school	149 (49.66%)	151 (50.33%)
Reading habit in the school library	41 (13.66%)	259 (86.33%)
Going to school all times during a year	163 (54.33%)	137 (45.66%)

It is observed from the above table that only 49.66 per cent of Namasudra students are getting books and economical help from their school, but majority of the students' i.e. 50.33 per cent are not getting any books or any financial help from the school. The reading percentage in library in West Bengal is too worse. The report reveals that only 13.66 per cent of students can read in the school library, but majority i.e. 86.33 per cent of Namasudra students do not study habit in the school library in the state. So far as the socio-economic problems of this group of people, maximum of them are unable to avail the school time regularly. It is reveals from the table that 54.33 per cent of this group of people can go to the school regularly in all seasons of year, but 45.66 per cent of students are not able to go the school regularly due to various reasons, as a result more drop out and stagnation problems occurred in this group of people in both the states.

Teacher Related Problems: In teaching learning process of present education system, teachers play a very great role. In the traditional system of education the learners remains in the classes as the passive learner. So, their learning is totally depending on the teacher's teaching, which generally taking place in the classroom. In this regard every student should become very careful as well as conscious enough to listen the teaching given by the teacher. But in this regard some students get problem from the teacher, due to which they remain lagging behind than the other students. Few of such problems and students response are mentioned in Table 6.7.

Data analysis made in the above table that Namasudra students of West Bengal face more problems in understanding the lessons taught by the teachers. The table shows that 84.33 per cent of students can understand the teaching given by the teacher in the class; and 15.66 per cent of students do not understand the teaching given by the teacher. This

Table 6.7: Teacher related Problems Faced by the Namasudra Students

Nature of Problems	*West Bengal*	
Understanding the teaching of the teacher	253 (84.33%)	47 (15.66%)
Teachers helping hand in the study	300 (100%)	0
Doing the home works in given time	287 (95.66%)	13 (4.33%)
Conversation freely with the teachers	254 (84.66%)	46 (15.33%)
Perception of the language of the teachers	294 (98%)	6 (2%)
Asking questions to the teachers in the classroom	264 (88%)	36 (12%)

group of people faces a lot of problems in their learning, and as a result they fall under drop out and stagnation problem. Again it is observed from the above table that in West Bengal 100 per cent students get all sorts of help from the teacher regarding the study. It is reported in the table that 95.66 per cent SC students of West Bengal do their home in right time, and 4.33 per cent students do not do their home work in due time. 84.66 per cent of student of this group can talk freely with the teacher in the school in West Bengal. But 15.33 per cent students face the problem of conversation with their teacher. Regarding the medium of instruction the state having fewer problems so far the table report is concerned. Only 2 per cent students in West Bengal are facing the language problem. This is may be due to the teacher's way of expression and clear voice problem.

Reading Related Problems: Reading related problems generally hamper the students in their study at home. These problems generally generate at the home, for which family members, family environment, family cooperation, family motivation, encouragement and financial factors of the family are responsible. If a student faces above mentioned factors in his/her home than definitely study of that particular students will be affected very badly, and consequently the students may fall under either drop out or stagnation problem. So far the above mention factors are concerned the Namasudra students are being affected mostly in the rural areas in the state, which have been observed from the field visit by the researcher. Some problems regarding these and respondents response is shown Table 6.8.

Data analysis made in the above table shows that the good numbers of students from West Bengal are not getting necessary books required for study. It is found that 41.66 per cent of Namasudra students are not having necessary books require for their study. It shows that majority of this group of peoples in the state are studying in school are without necessary books at their home. If such is the situation prevailing in the state than what result may be expected from them.

Table 6.8: Problem related to Books/Home Tutor/Guardians and Family

Nature of Problems	*West Bengal*	
	Yes	No
Necessary books require for your study	175 (58.33%)	125 (41.66%)
Extending help by members of family in study	133 (44.33%)	167 (55.66%)
Compulsion by parents to do domestic works without allowing for study	15 (5%)	285 (95%)
Home tutor for help in your study	210 (70%)	90 (30%)

The Namasudra students of West Bengal have to face the study related problem. It's found that around 55.66 per cent of this group student does not have any individual in their home to help in their study. This condition usually hampers the students study in their home. Again, in the state it is found that 95 per cent students belong to Namasudra community agreed that their parent do not make them compel to do their domestic work instead reading at home.

A section of students from the state replied that they read in their home without tutor. Now a days, it has become a fashion to have tutor at home to get help in their study. Due to this fashion only some students read at home and some do not. The report reveals that 70 per cent students have home tutor at their home, and 30 per cent of them do not have this facility.

Table 6.9: Time Expend in Studies by the Namasudra Students in both the States

State	*½ Hour*	*1 or 2 hour*	*2 to 3 hour*	*3 to 4 or more*
West Bengal	9 (3%)	39 (13%)	124 (41.33%)	128 (42.66%)

It is revealed from the above table that around 42.66 per cent Namasudra students of the state are expending 3 to 4 hours per day for their study purpose. Again 41.33 per cent spends 2 to 3 hours, 13 per cent spends 1 to 2 hours and only 3 per cent students of this category spend only ½ hour time in their study. From this table it may be concluded that the habit of study in West Bengal among Namasudras is seems to be good. This will enhance their performance level in the school and they can compete with others (*see* Fig. 6.1).

Table 6.10: Lighting Source Used at Night by the Namasudra Students

State	*Kerosene light*	*Electric light*	*Street light*
West Bengal	83 (27.66%)	213 (71%)	4 (1.33%)

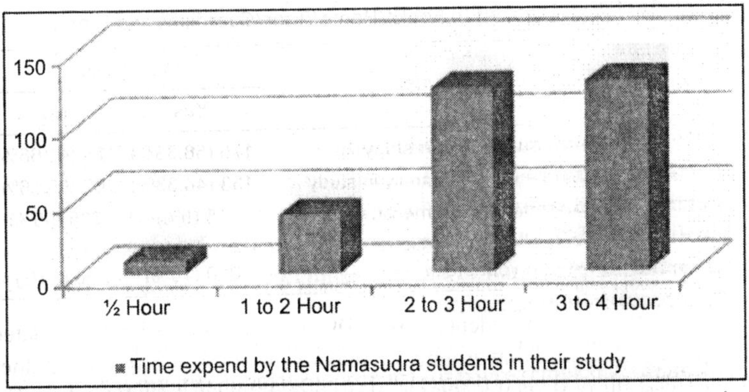

Fig. 6.1: Graphical Representation of Time Expend in Study by the Namasudra Students in the State

From the Table 6.10 it is found that the students of West Bengal getting better facilities at night in their reading. It is reveal that 71 per cent Namasudra students in West Bengal are using Electric light at night for their reading purpose, and only 27.66 per cent students of the state are using kerosene light at night in their reading purpose. Its' also found that 1.33 per cent Namasudra students of West Bengal are still using street light in the state

Table 6.11: Self Understanding the Subject Matter by the Namasudra Students

State	*Yes*	*No*
West Bengal	140 (46.66%)	160 (53.33%)

The data analyzed above reveals that a good number of Namasudra students do not understand the subject matter of their course by self reading in the state. As it is mentioned earlier that good number of students in the state do not have home tutor at home to help them in their study. As they do not have home tutor so, they have to understand the content at home by their self study. But the above table reveals that 53.33 per cent students of West Bengal are facing this problem. On the other hand only 46.66 per cent Namasudra students of West Bengal understand the course content by self reading at their home. Thus, it is emerge from the statement that majority of the students in the state are suffering from this problem.

1. General Problem: General problem comprises all sorts of problems which are related to the factors which have been mentioned above. This problem may be categorized as miscellaneous problem. The problems coming under this category have been shown in Table 6.12.

Table 6.12: Parent's Education of Namasudra Students in West Bengal

State	*Educated*	*Uneducated*	*Semi-literate*
West Bengal	74 (24.66)	52 (17.33)	174 (58%)

It is found from the above table that the educational status of Namasudra parents in the state. It is reported that only 24.66 per cent parents of West Bengal are educated. Again it is noticed from the above table that 17.33 per cent parents of West Bengal are uneducated. It is also found that large section of the Namasudra people i.e. 58 per cent in the state are only functional literate.

Table 6.13: Problems related to School Subject/Examination/Books

Nature of Problems	*West Bengal*	
	Yes	No
Necessity of every subject of school	294 (98%)	6 (2%)
Lack of time for study during examination	80 (26.66%)	220 (73.33%)
Able to buy books whenever necessary	108 (36%)	192 (64%)

The above table reveals that 98 per cent Namasudra students of West Bengal agreed that every subject of school is important, and only 2 per cent students from West Bengal do not support of having every subject in the school which is existing at present. Again it is reveals from the above table that 26.66 per cent students of West Bengal feel inconvenient to study for more time during the examination. Either due to their pressure of domestic works or due to lack of support from the family they are not getting sufficient time to studies at home during period of examination. It is also found that 64 per cent Namasudra students of West Bengal are not able to purchase books required in their course of study whenever necessary. The above mentioned problems are very harmful problem to the students of any group, so whoever face such problem definitely his/her study will be affected. So, these problems should not allow entering among the students.

Table 6.14: Problems related to School Going and Domestic Works

Nature of Problems	West Bengal	
	Yes	No
Regularity in the school	166 (55.33%)	134 (44.66%)
Going to school only after doing domestic works	96 (32%)	204 (68%)

The above table again reveals that 44.66 per cent students of West Bengal cannot go to the school regularly due to certain causes. If such a big number of student do not go to the school every day than how they will continue their study, and one can expect better education status from any state. Again, it is observed from the above table that maximum students of the state go to the school after doing their domestic at their home. It is generally happen among the backward class communities' people in other states also. It is found from the report that 32 per cent students go the school after doing the domestic works at home.

Table 6.15: Problems related to Finance of the Study

Nature of Problems	*West Bengal*	
	Yes	*No*
Earn by self employment for study	115 (38.33%)	185 (61.66%)
Getting scholarship for scheduled caste in time	151 (50.33%)	149 (49.66%)

As it is found from the various sources that the Namasudra people living in the state are very poor, so far their socio-economic status is concerned. As a result the students of this community are facing a lot of problem regarding their educational aspects. It is found from the above table that 38.33 per cent students of under this community in West Bengal are continuing their study from their own income made from different sources. Again it is reveals from the above table that in the state students expressed that almost 49.33 per cent of students are not getting scholarships at time from their school which is meant for scheduled caste students. It may be the government's fault due to which they are not getting the same at the proper time.

Table 6.16: Problems related to Food and Society

Nature of Problems	*West Bengal*	
	Yes	*No*
Nutritious food required for reading	144 (48%)	156 (52%)
Criticizing study by other caste people in the society	189 (63%)	111 (37%)

The students of West Bengal are not getting nutritious food from their family which is require for their study, so far the above mentioned report is concerned. It is found from the above table that 52 per cent students of the state are still not getting nutritious food required for their study. If the majority students do not get proper food/nutritious food than what education may be expected from them. Because for education of a child, good health is necessary, good health is depends on good/nutritious food taken by the child.

Again from the above table it is observed that a good number of students in the state are facing one very acute problem, which should not faced by the said group people, so far the development of the society is concerned. Majority of the students in the state are being criticized by the people belong to other caste of the society. It is very unfortunate that our India is democratic country, where every individual should get equal right and facility from the government, there should not be any discrimination in the society. But there are some people living in our society, they are belong to so called higher caste and they criticize the lower caste people, and one of such as victim group is Namasudras in the society. It is reveal from the above table prepared from the response given the students from the state that around 63 per cent students of state reported that they are being criticized by their society because of their schooling. It is a very unfortunate that a large number of students are facing this problem in the state.

ATTITUDE TOWARD EDUCATION OF NAMASUDRA STUDENTS

It is found from the various studies and observations that the Namasudra people living in the state West Bengal are less conscious and having less favourable attitudes towards education. So far the educational process is concerned; education of a child depends on various factors, which influences to the child's education. Education of an individual seeks cooperation from students, parent/guardians and community members of the society. Hence, the present researcher has initiated to find out the level of attitudes towards education from all these section of the society to see the feeling, interest and views about education of the people of this particular community. In the present section the researcher has gathered information about the attitudes of Namasudra students, parent and community members towards education. From the field visit it has been observed that these groups of people are living in the backward areas, which affects in their living style and attitudes, interests, thinking, reasoning and any other psychological aspect of an individual. An attitude of an individual gets influenced through their socio-economic condition, living style and the environment where he/she is grown up. If somebody lives in very high socio-economic condition, than definitely his/her mental attitude towards different things will be far above the ground; in the same way if someone lives in very poor socio-economic condition than his thinking, reasoning, attitude and other things will be in that category level. In the present study an attitude regarding education has been collected through an attitude scale developed by the researchers themselves.

It has already been mentioned that people's attitude towards education has a great role, whether they will go for education or facilitate their children to have education. Favourable attitude induces the individual to have their own education or, they will suggest other to have education and vise versa. From the Table 6.17 it's make to known that the 93.33 per cent of students of West Bengal belong to Namasudra community has their average level favourable attitude towards education. This will promote the students to have further education in their life. On the other hand only 6.67 per cent of students of this community in West Bengal has highly favourable attitude toward education. It is found from the field observation that the people under this community are come to school from very poor socio-economic conditions. It's also found from the same study that most of them are illiterate and functional literate. The children form their interest, attitude and concept in the influences of family environment. It's found from the observation that 17.33 per cent parents are illiterate and 58 per cent parents are semi-literate, these conditions of the people endorses to have a unfortunate kind of attitude towards education in their life.

Table 6.17: Level of Attitudes of the Namasudra Students toward Education

Level of attitudes	*Ranges of the scores*	*frequency*	*Percentage*
High level favourable attitude	130-192	280	93.33%
Average level favourable attitude	65-129	20	6.67%
Poor level attitude	0-64	0	0.00%
		Total= 300	

On the other hand the Table 6.18 reveals that 83.67 per cent community members have high level favourable attitude towards education. Again, only 16.33 per cent community member have average level attitude towards education. Here the community members of Namasudra category are more aware and having high level favourable attitude towards education, because these people have gone through different types of knowledge and experiences in their life and they have

Table 6.18: Level of Attitudes of the Namasudra Community Members toward Education

Level of attitudes	*Ranges of the scores*	*frequency*	*percentage*
High level favourable attitude	102-152	251	83.67%
Average level favourable attitude	51-101	49	16.33%
Poor level attitude	0-50	0	0.00%
		Total= 300	

realized the actual need of education in the human life for development of the personality and the community as a whole.

Table 6.19: Level of Attitudes of the Namasudra Parents toward Education

Level of attitudes	*Ranges of the scores*	*frequency*	*percentage*
High level favourable attitude	108-160	249	83%
Average level favourable attitude	54-107	51	17%
Poor level attitude	0-53	0	0.00%
		Total= 300	

Again from the above table it is found that 83 per cent of the Namasudra parents have their high level favourable towards education and 17 per cent parents have average level attitude towards education about their children. In comparison to the community member of the same group, the parent has similar kind of attitude of attitudes. In fact the parents should have the highest level attitude in comparison to the any member of the community. From the data reveal from the above table it can be concluded that the parent of the Namasudra people have high level attitude towards their children education.

Table 6.20: 'T' Test regarding the Attitude towards Education between Namasudra Students and Parents

Group	*N*	*Mean*	*S.D.*	*ΔD*	*CR*	*Df*	*Significant of*	
Students	300	146.48	20.99	1.35	22.25	598	5%	1%
Parents	300	116.44	10.31				1.96	2.58

The above table reveals that the attitudes towards education of Namasudra students and parents have quite differences. The Mean value of the students and Parents has reasonably differences i.e. 30.04. The calculation reveals that the standard error of difference is 1.35 and critical ratio or Z value is 22.25. With df 598 it is found from the table that the calculated value i.e. CR = 22.25 is quite larger than the table value 1.96 at 5 per cent level and 2.58 at 1 per cent level of significance. Hence, we may accept the null hypothesis in both level and may be concluded that the difference between students and parents regarding the attitudes towards education is a true difference.

Table 6.21: 'T' Test regarding the Attitude towards Education between Namasudra Students and Community Members

Group	*N*	*Mean*	*S.D.*	*ΔD*	*CR*	*df*	*Significant of*	
Students	300	146.48	20.99	1.93	18.20	598	5%	1%
Community Members	300	111.34	11.79				1.96	2.58

It is revealed from the Table 6.21 that the Namasudra students and community members of West Bengal have their difference level of attitude towards education. It is found from the report that Namasudra students of West Bengal has more favourable attitude than the any other group including. The data mentioned above reveals that the Mean difference between student and community members is 35.14, and the standard error of difference is 1.93. After calculation it is found that the Z value or the Critical value is 18.20, which is quite larger than the table in both levels of significance. Hence, the null hypothesis is accepted in both level of significance, and it may be concluded that the difference between Namasudra students and Namasudra community members is a true difference.

Table 6.22: 'T' Test regarding the Attitude towards Education between Namasudra Parents and Community Members

Group	*N*	*Mean*	*S.D.*	*?D*	*CR*	*Df*	*Significant of*	
Parents	300	116.44	10.31	0.90	5.66	598	5%	1%
Community Members	300	111.34	11.79				1.96	2.58

The above table reveals that the attitudes towards education of Namasudra parents and community members have quite differences. It's found that the community members and parents of Namasudra students have almost same level of attitude towards education in state. The Mean value of the parents and community members has reasonably differences i.e. 5.1. The calculation reveals that the standard error of difference is 0.90 and critical ratio or Z value is 5.66. With df 598 it is found from the table that the calculated value i.e. CR = 5.66 is quite larger than the table value 1.96 at 5 per cent level and 2.58 at 1 per cent level of significance. Hence, we may accept the null hypothesis in both level and may be concluded that the difference between Namasudra parents and community members regarding the attitudes towards education is a true difference.

Suggestion to the Namasudra Students in West Bengal for their Equitable Participation in Education

It is found from the above discussion made in the Section—I, II, III and IV that the Namasudra students in state are backward in their field of education in comparison to many other caste people of the state. Besides, the Namasudra students face lot of problem in their study life in the state. It also found from the above discussion that this group of people are backward in other filed also due to which they are unable to continue their study for long time. Again they have number of problem in their life which impacts their children's education. In this regard though government has taken some initiatives but the objectives of all those step is still yet to fulfillment. Education is the only means of development of any country or state. So for equitable participation in education following suggestion may be provided.

- For active participation of Namasudra people in education, it is urgently required to improve the economic condition of Namasudra families as the financial problem is the major problem in perusing education by them.
- It is necessary and urgent to make the parents understand about the importance of education: enrolment and continuation of study, at any cost by their children. In this mission the Govt. support system, N.G.O.s, schools and teachers have to be inter linked and they have to work under a common monitoring system.
- Another strategy may be the establishment of linkages between schools and the community. Improvement of parents-teacher association is necessary and essential. This is important to increase the attendance of Namasudra students in school.
- Close collaboration among concerned entities like schools; government and non govt. agencies, parents and teachers; teachers and community; schools within an area may be one of the most significant driving force.

- Convening small workshops at the community level by the concerned authorities or individual to inform the community about various Govt. funds and schemes provided for scheduled castes in education may be an effective strategy.
- Involvement of teachers, head of the institution and community members is important in the planning of any educational programme provided for that particular locality.
- Govt. and non-government agencies along with the community members have to work together to check the over population in most of the scheduled caste families. This will unload the financial pressure from those families.
- It is essential and urgent to reduce or stop the misappropriation of various Govt. funds and schemes provided for the scheduled caste students.
- Appointment of educated and eligible scheduled caste individuals in Govt. or non-govt. job is necessary, especially in teaching and if so, those teachers are to be appointed in their local area. Job aspirations among the scheduled caste are to be increased.
- Every individual or agency or authority is to be honest in their work in this mission. Authorities have to give importance on the practical work on the field but not in the paper work.
- Some sort of guidance and counseling may be arranged for the Namasudra parents to make them aware about the importance of education in life, so that they can understand their responsibilities of provide all arrangement for their child's education.
- Special scheme may be introduced to make more enrolment of rural scheduled caste students in the school.
- Special incentive to those below the poverty level and engaged mostly as agricultural labourers, subsistence farmers, artisans, collectors of minor forest produce and urban slum dwellers to enlist and sustain their children for compulsory education.
- Payment of cash compensation in the form of opportunity cost to those parents who for economic and social constraints cannot send their children to schools.
- Schemes like payment of monthly stipend to child labourers, pre-matric scholarships to children of those who are living in the below poverty level.
- Establishment of educational institutions in rural areas in such a manner that they are within easy reach of the below poverty level people or downtrodden people.

- Study centers and reading rooms within easy reach of students' residences should be provided. Some class rooms of the school may be kept open during early morning and late evening hours for the benefit of those students who do not have suitable place to study at home.
- Extra coaching classes should be organized free of cost for the deficient students during week-ends and holidays.
- Extra-curricular activities should be strengthened in schools and all the students should be encouraged to participate more and more actively.
- There should be time bound programme of free compulsory literacy and free elementary education for all people. This will open the gates of education, progress and prosperity to all people. Free and quality education will ensure equal opportunities for all, without restriction, enabling everyone to fight for self esteem and progress.
- Special efforts should be made to draw the scheduled caste students from their homes into hostels where the best of education be given for those who lag behind.
- More, better and cheaper hostel facilities for the scheduled caste students should be provided.
- The hostel superintendent should be such as would be able to take on the role of parents in supervising, directing, guiding and counseling the scheduled caste students in performing their student's role.
- The minimum amount of scholarships should be increased. The amount of the scholarship should be granted starting from the minimum so that the students showing better results get more.
- The formal procedure of securing benefits should be simplified as much as possible.
- Provision of benefits to the scheduled caste students should be so devised as to encourage merit. Incentives should be provided for those show greater merit.
- Instead of providing a lower limit for admission to educational institutions, remedial measures should be organized and implemented to raise their level of performance.
- Talented scheduled caste students to be spotted from class V and the state should take full responsibility of their education up to a certain level, say up to the higher secondary level. These students should get the best of education in best environment

with proper emphasis for their physical, mental and cultural development.

- Teachers of the school belong to non-scheduled caste community should be impartial and very liberal toward the students. No students belong to scheduled caste community should feel that they are being criticized by the teachers in the school because of low status in the society.
- Teachers in the school should be very accessible to the students, so that they can approach freely with their teachers in the school whenever necessary.
- Extra care should be taken by the teachers to the scheduled caste students in their study in the school, because they coming from very low and poor family background.
- To improve the participation of scheduled caste/Namasudra people in education the government should improve the communication facility in the areas where the scheduled caste people are living. Then only they will be able to come to the school every day.
- Infrastructure condition of the school should be attractive to the scheduled caste, and sitting arrangement and other necessary arrangement should be made properly.
- Concession should be given to the scheduled caste people in tuition fee and other necessary fees of the school.
- Government may introduce the facility to provide dress and other necessary things to the scheduled caste people to meet up their basic needs required for their study.
- Study environment should be made properly by the parents and guardians of schedule caste people for study at home. When they will study properly at home than there will be problem of wastage and stagnation in the school.
- School environment of the school should be attractive to the children, so that they may prefer to go the school than stay at home.
- Attempt should be made to make the parents and guardians conscious enough, that their children should go to the school regularly instead of doing domestic work at the home.
- Through adult education policy, illiterate scheduled caste parents and guardians should be educated enough to understand the value and necessity of education for their children.

- Child labour should completely be stopped among scheduled caste community, and at the same time education should be fundamental right to all children for the age of 6-14 years.
- Article No. 14 of the Indian Constitution should be implemented properly in practically also.
- Proper study environment as well as sitting arrangement for study at home should be made available for the scheduled caste children, than only they will be interested to go the school regularly.
- Scholarship given for the scheduled caste students should be made regular to the all scheduled caste people in the school.
- Books and other materials such as pen, paper, pencil and slate should be given free to the scheduled caste students up to secondary level of education.
- Government may made provision for summer school, winter school and special coaching for scheduled caste students at completely free of cost.
- Free electricity facility to the scheduled caste students at least one light may be given to the poor scheduled caste students to read at night.
- Educational institutions should be established in the scheduled caste areas.
- The rural scheduled caste people are more poor, so they should be given much emphasis in case of providing facilities.
- Caste system should be abolished.
- More emphasis should be given on the educational facilities of these people.
- Government should try to establish socialism in the country.
- Government should adopt large scale schemes for the development scheduled caste and tribes.
- Government should try to be careful so that high caste people can't introduce themselves as scheduled caste people to accept facilities.
- Government should try to establish equality and fraternity in the society.
- Compulsory system of education up to high school level should be arranged.
- Some students from among scheduled caste/tribe should be sent abroad for acquiring higher education and training.
- Adult education should be encouraged to motivate the parents and guardians regarding education.

- Residential type of education may be arranged in the scheduled caste areas.
- Practical programmes in education, like sanitations, health education, and cottage industry should be adopted in the institutions for them.
- More teachers should be appointed from the scheduled caste groups in those areas.
- Education should be job-oriented for the scheduled caste.
- There should be a separate Directorate of Education to proper attention to the scheduled caste in both the states.

Bibliography

Aberle, Devid F. (1961), "Culture and Socialization" in *Psychological Anthropology—Approaches to culture and Personality*, Dorsey Press; Home Wood, pp. 381-399.

Adaval, S.B.Ed. (1968), Third Indian Yearbook of Education; Educational Research; NCERT; New Delhi.

Aggarwal, Y. and Sibou, S. (1994), *Educating Scheduled Castes: A Study of Inter District and Intra Caste Differentials*, NIEPA, New Delhi.

Anderson, J.B. *et al.* (1971), *Thesis and Assignment Writing*, Wiley Eastern Limited; New Delhi.

Assam. Govt. (1961), *Scheduled Caste and Scheduled Tribes*; Vol. 4; Part 5 (A); Manager of Publications, New Delhi.

Ausubol, David, P. (1968), *Educational Psychology, A Cognitive View*; Holt. Rinehard and Winston, Inc; New York.

Babbie, E.R. (1973), *Survey Research Methods*; Calif. Wardsworth Publishing Co; Belmont.

Bag, D.C. (1984), *Impact of Education on some Backward Communities of West Bengal: Study based on West Dinajpur*, DPS Publisher, Calcutta.

Bandyopadhyay, S. and *et al.* (1994), *Bengal Communities Development and States*, Mohohar publishers, Delhi.

Bandyopadhyay, S. (1994), Development, Differentiation and Caste: The Namasudra movement in Bengal, 1872-1947, *Bengal Communities Development and States* (Ed.), S. Bandypadhyay and *et al.*, Mohohar publishers, Delhi.

Banerjee, M. (1954), *Primitive Man in India*; India Publications; Ambala Cant.

Banton, Michael (1968), *International Encyclopedia of Social Sciences*; Vol. 1-6; Macmillan; New York.

Bareja, J.D. (1982), *New Horizons of North East*; Western Book Depot, Guwahati.

Best, J.W. (1982), *Research in Education*; Prentice Hall of India Pvt. Ltd.; New Delhi.

Bhandari, R.K. and Khurana, G.A. (1978), Study of Administrative Set Up in States for Educational Programmes of Scheduled Castes and Scheduled Tribes, Ministry of Education and Social Welfare, Planning, Monitoring and Statistics Division, New Delhi.

Bharadwaj, A.N. (1979), *Problems of Schedule Castes and Scheduled Tribes in India*, Light and Life Publishers, New Delhi.

Bhatia, S.C. (1982), *Education and Socio-Cultural Disadvantage*, Xerxex Publications, Delhi.

Bhuimali, A. (2007), *Development of Scheduled Caste*, Serials Publications, New Delhi.

Biswas, A.K. (2000), *The Namasudra of Bengal*, Blumoon Books, New Delhi.

Biswas, U.N. (2004), *The Strike*, NCMB Memorial Trust, Kolkata.

Buch, M.B. (1986), *Third Survey of Educational Research*, (1978-83), NCERT, New Delhi.

Buch, M.B. Ed (1974), *A Survey of Research in Education*; CASE; M.S. University; Baroda.

Buch, M.B. Ed. (1979), *Second Survey of Research in Education (1972-1978)*, Society for Educational Research and Development; Baroda.

Buch, M.B. Ed. (1987), *Third Survey of Research in Education*, NCERT; New Delhi.

Buch, M.B., (1991), *Fourth Survey of Educational Research*, (1983-88), Vol. I and II, NCERT, New Delhi.

Campbell, W.G. (1969), Form and Style of Thesis Writing; Houghton Mifflin Company; Boston.

Census of India, Final Population Totals (1991), Paper 1 of 1992, Vol. I; Manager of Publications; New Delhi.

Census of India, Scheduled Castes and Scheduled Tribe Population in Census of India, 1993; paper-I, Registrar General and Census Commissioner; India.

Chalam, K.S. (1988), *Education and Weaker Section*, Inter India, New Delhi.

Chalam, K.S. (1988), *Education and Weaker Sections*; Inter India Publications; New Delhi.

Chatterjee, S.K. (1996), *The Scheduled Caste in India*, Gyan Publishing House, New Delhi.

Chatterjee, S.K. (2000), *Educational Development of Scheduled Caste—Looking Ahed*, Gyan Publishing House, New Delhi.

Chauhan, B.R. (1967), "Special Problems of the Education of the Scheduled castes", in M.S. Gore, I.P. Desai and S. Chitnis (Eds.), Papers in *Sociology of Education in India*, NCERT, New Delhi.

Chauhan, B.R. *et al.* (1975). *Scheduled Castes and Education*, Anu Publication, Meerut.

Chitnis, S. (1974). First Survey in Social Sciences; ICSSR; New Delhi.

Chitnis, S. (1978), Education of the Scheduled Castes and Scheduled Tribes in Maharashtra, in *The Social Context of Education*, Edited by A.B. Shah, Allied Publishers, New Delhi.

Chitnis, S. (1981), *A Long Way to Go: Report on a Survey of Scheduled Caste High School and College Students in 15 States of India*, Allied Publishers, New Delhi.

Chitnis, S., *Literacy and Educational Enrolment among the Scheduled Castes of Maharashtra*, Tata Institute of Social Sciences, Bombay.

D'Souza, V.S. (1980), *Educational Inequalities Among Scheduled Castes: A Case Study in the Punjab*, Punjab University, Chandigarh.

Dalton, Edward Tuite (1872), *Descriptive Ethnology of Bengal*; Govt. Printing Press; Calcutta.

Das, A.K. *et al.* (1966), *Handbook on Scheduled Castes and Scheduled Tribes of West Bengal*; Tribal Welfare Department; Govt. of West Bengal; Calcutta.

Das, B.M. (1987), *The People of Assam*, Gyan Publishing House, Delhi.

Doly, N.Y. 91971), *Isolation of Backward Community Students*; Janata Publishing Co. New Delhi.

Dubey, S.N. (1973), *Administration of Social Welfare Programmes for Backward Classes in India*, Somaiya Publications, New Delhi.

Dugdale, K. (1967), A manual Writing Research; Indian University Book Store; Indiana.

Dutta, N.K. (1986), *Origin and growth of Caste in India*, KLM, Calcutta.

Ebel, R.L. (Ed.) (1969), *Encyclopedia of Educational Research*; The Macmillan Co.; London.

Edwards, A.L. (1957), *Techniques of Attitude Scale Construction; Appleton Century Crofts*; Inc; New York.

Festinger, L. *et al.* (1970), *Research Methods in Behavioural Sciences*; Amerind Publishing Co. Pvt. Ltd; New Delhi.

Fox, D.J. (1969), *The Research Process in Education*; Holt Rinehart and Winston; New York.

Francis, K. (1993), *Education and Development*; Discovery Publishing House; New Delhi.

Freeman, F.S. (1965), *Theory and Practice of Psychological Testing*; Oxford IBH Publishing Co.; New Delhi.

Freeman, F.S. (1971), *Theory and Practice of Psychological Testing*; (3rd Indian Edition), IBH Publishing Co.; Bombay.

Garrett, H.E. (1962), *Statistics in Psychology and Education*; Allied Pacific Private Ltd.; Bombay.

Ghurye, G.S. (1996), *Caste and Race in India*, Popular Prakashan, Bombay.

Good, C.V. Ed. (1959), *Dictionary of Education*; Mc Graw Hill Book Company; New York.

Good, C.V. *et al.* (1941), *Methodology of Educational Research*; Appleton-Century Crofts Inc.; New York.

Good, W.J. *et al.* (1952), *Methods in Social Research*, Mc. Graw Hill Book Company; New York.

Govt. of India (1961), *West Bengal and Sikkim: Special Tables Scheduled Tribes*, Vol. 16, Part 5(A), No. 2; Manager of Publications; New Delhi.

Govt. of India (1966), *Report of the Education Commission*, 1964-66. Ministry of Education and Culture.

Govt. of India (1983), *A Handbook of Educational and Allied Statistics*; Ministry of Education and Culture, New Delhi.

Govt. of India (1984), *Analysis of Budgeted Expenditure on Education, 1981-82 to 1983-84*; Ministry of Education and Culture New Delhi.

Govt. of India (1984), *Selected Educational Statistics, 1982-83*; Ministry of Education and Culture, New Delhi.

Govt. of India (1985), *Challenge of Education: A Policy Perspective; Ministry of Human Resource Development*, New Delhi.

Govt. of India (1986), *National Policy on Education*; Ministry of Human Resource Development, New Delhi.

Govt. of India (1986), *Programme of Action; Action; Ministry of Human Resource Development*, New Delhi.

Govt. of India (1975), *Schedules Castes and Schedules Tribes*; Series 1. Paper 1 of 1975; Manager of publications; New Delhi.

Govt. of India (1982), West Bengal: Final population Table; Total Population, Scheduled Castes and Scheduled Tribe Population, in *Census of India*; 1981, Series 23, paper 1 of 1982; Director of Census operations, Calcutta.

Govt. of India, (1981), Primary Census Abstract of Scheduled Castes and Scheduled Tribes, *Census of India*, Series 4, Paper 2 of 1982; Controller of Publications; New Delhi.

Govt. of India, Constitution of India.

Goyal, B.R. (1981): *Educating Harijans*, Academics, Gurgaon.

Hanumantha and Mutharayappa (1986), *Backwardness and Welfare of Scheduled Caste and Scheduled Tribes in India*, Ashish Publishing, New Delhi.

Harros Chester, W. Ed. (1960), *Encyclopedia of Research*; Mc Graw Hill, New York.

Hasnain, N. (1991), *Tribal India Today*, Harnam Publication, New Delhi.

Hasnain, Nadeem (1986), *Tribal India Today*; Harnam Publications; New Delhi.

Haviland, W.A. (1990), *Cultural Anthropology*; Holt, Rinehart and Winston, Inc.; Orland; USA.

Hers Kovits, M.J. (1964), *Cultural Dynamics*; New York.

Hilway, Tyrus (1964), *Introduction to Research*; Houghton Mifflin Company; Boston.

Jha, M.L. (1973), *Untouchability and Education: A Sociological Study of Attitudes*, Namita Publications; Meerut.

Johnson, Palmar, O. (1961), *Statistical Method of Research*, Asia Publishing; New Delhi.

Kabra, L. (1991), *Scheduled Caste Girls*, Mittal; New Delhi.

Kamble, N.D. (1981), *Atrocities on Scheduled Castes in the Post-Independence India (15th August 1947 to 15th August 1979)*: Ashish Publishing House; New Delhi.

Karlekar, M. (1983), 'Education and Inequality', in Andre Beteille (Ed.), *Equality and Inequality*: Oxford University Press; Delhi.

Karlinger, F.N. (1978), Foundations of

Ketkar, S.V. (1979), *The History of Caste in India*, Cosmo Publications, New Delhi, India.

Khan, M.A. (1975), *Research on Development of Scheduled Castes*: Vikash; Delhi.

Khan, M.A. (1980), *Scheduled Castes and their Status in India*: Uppal; New Delhi.

Koul, L. (1984), *Methodology of Educational Research* (Reprint 1999); Vikas Publishing House; New Delhi.

Kulashrestha, S.P. (1979), *Educational Psychology*; International Publishing House; Meerut; U.P.

Kundu, C.L. (1976), *Educational Psychology*; Sterling Publishers Pvt. Ltd., New Delhi.

Laha, S.S. and Bhuimali, A. (2007), Genesis of Scheduled Castes and Constitutional Safeguards for them, (Ed) *Development of Scheduled Caste, Anil Bhuimali,* Serial Publications, New Delhi.

Lal, S.K. and U.R. Nahar (1978), *Higher Education: Scheduled Castes and Scheduled Tribes*; Jainsons, Jodhpur.

Lal, S.K., *et al.* (1978), *Higher Education: Scheduled Castes and Scheduled Tribes*, Jainsons, Jodhpur.

Lalnithanga, P. (1988), "Special Tables for Scheduled Castes and Scheduled Tribes" in *Census of India*, 1981; Controller of Publications; New Delhi.

Lokshmanna, C., *et al.* (1977), *Depressed Group Students: Between Yesterday and Tomorrow*, College Book House, Trivandrum.

Mackenzie, A. (Reprint 1979), *The North-East Frontier of India*; Mittal Publications; New Delhi.

Malik, S. (1971), *Social Integration of Scheduled Castes*, Abhinav Publications, New Delhi.

McDonald, J. and Gibson, C.C. (1988), *Fifth Survey of Educational Research* (1988-92), NCERT, New Delhi.

Ministry of Education (1985), *Educational Facilities to Scheduled Castes and Scheduled Tribes*, Planning Monitoring and Statistics Division, Scheduled Castes and Scheduled Tribes Cell, Ministry of Education, New Delhi.

N.C.E.R.T. (1982), *Fourth All India Educational Survey*; N.C.E.R.T.; New Delhi.

Naik, J.P. (1971), *Education of the Scheduled Tribes*, ICSSR, New Delhi.

Naik, J P. (1972), *Education of the Scheduled Castes*, ICSSR, New Delhi.

Naik, J.P. (1972), *Education of the Scheduled Castes and Scheduled Tribes*, The Manager of Publications, New Delhi.

O'Donnell, C.J. (1893), *Lower Provinces of Bengal 1891*; Calcutta.

Om, P.S. (1986), *Caste and Politics in Indian Education*, Deep and Deep, New Delhi.

Pandey, P.N. (1988), *Education and Social Mobility*, Daya Publishing House, Delhi.

Parvathamma, C.S. (1984), *New Horizons and Scheduled Castes*, Ashish, New Delhi.

Paswan, S. and *et al.* (2004), *Encyclopedia of Dalit in India Social Justice*, Kalpaz Publications, Delhi.

Patel, T. (1984), *Development of Education Among Tribal Women*, Mittal, Delhi.

Patwardhan, S. (1973), *Change Among Indian Harijans: Maharashtra: A Case Study*, Orient Longman, New Delhi.

Pelto, P.J. (1993), *Anthropological Research the Structure of Inquiry*, Cambridge University Press.

Pimpley, P.N. (1980), *Profile of Scheduled Caste Students: the Case of Punjab*, Punjab University, Chandigarh.

Planning Commission, (1982), Programme Evalution Division, Study of Post-Matric Scholarship Scheme for Scheduled Castes and Scheduled Tribes: Report Survey (July-August, 1980), New Delhi.

Premi, K.K. (1989), *Scheduled Castes and Scheduled Tribes in Industrial Training Institutes: A Study of Five States*, Vikash Publishing House, New Delhi.

R.G.I. (2001), Census of India.

Radhakrishnan, S. and Ranjana, K. (1989), *Impact of Education on Scheduled Caste Youth in India*; Radiant Publishers, New Delhi.

Rangari, A.D. (1984), *Indian Caste System and Education*; Deep and Deep, New Delhi.

Rao, G.H. (1977), *Caste and Poverty: A Case Study of Scheduled Castes in a Delta Village*; Savithri Pulications.

Rao, R.S. (1989), *Caste System in India: Myth and Reality*, India Publishers and Distributors, New Delhi.

Rao, U. (1981), *Deprived Castes in India: A Profile of Karnataka*; Chugh Publications, Allahabad.

Ray, N.R. (1980), *Bengali Ithihas: Adi Parba*, Calcutta Niraksharata Durikaran Samiti, (3rd ed) Vol. I, Calcutta.

Rayappa, P. and *et al.* (1980), *Employment Planning for the Rural Poor: The Class of Schedule Castes and Scheduled Tribes*; Sterling Publications, New Delhi.

Raza and *et al.* (1982), *Reservation in Higher Education for Scheduled Castes and Scheduled Tribes: A Policy Framework*; NIEPA, New Delhi.

Risley, H.H. (1903), *Census of India*, 1901, Vol. I, Govt. of India, Calcutta.

Risley, H.H. (1998), Tribes and Castes of Bengal, *Ethnographic Glossary*, Firma KLM Private Limited, Calcutta. .

Roy, N. (), *History of the Bengali People*, Orient Langman,

Roy, R. (2000), Status of Tribal teachers in Assam and West Bengal: A Comparative Study, (Unpublished Ph.D Thesis).

Saksena, D. (1993), "The Socialisation of Critical Thought: Responses to Illiteracy Among the Adivasis in Thane District", pp. 85-112. In *Democracy and Education in India*, (Ed.) by Krishna Kumar; Radient Publications, New Delhi.

Sarkar, G. (1995), Jatitattwa Sangraha, (Bengali) Hiranmoy Sarkar, North 24 Paragana, West Bengal.

Sarkar, G. (1995), *Jatitattwa Sangraha, (Bengali) Hiranmoy Sarkar*, North 24 Paragana, West Bengal.

Sarkar, S. (1382, B Year), *Namasudrai Parsav Bipra*, Khulna Press, Khulna, Bagladesh.

Sarkar, S. (1382, Bengali Year), *Namasudrai Parsav Bipra*, Khulna Press, Khulna, Bagladesh.

Sarkar, S.R., *Namasudra Jatitattwa* (Bengali).

Sarkar, S.S. (1954), The Original Race of India, Book Land, Calcutta.

Seetharemu, A.S. (1983), *Education in Slums*; Ashish Publishing House.

Shah, V.P. (1975), *The Educational Problems of Scheduled Castes and Scheduled Tribes-School and College Students in India (A Statistics) Part-I*; Centre for Regional Development, Surat.

Sharma, K.L. (Ed) (2005), *Caste and Class in India*, Rawat Publications, Jaipur and New Delhi.

Showed, M. (1986), *Education and Mobility among Harijans*; Vohra Publishers, Varanasi.

Singh, K.S. (1995), *The Scheduled Castes*, Oxford University Press, Delhi.

Singh, K.S. (2008), *People of India, West Bengal*, Seagull Books, Calcutta.

Singh, K.S. (2008), *People of India, West Bengal*, Vol. XXXXIII, Anthropological Survey of India, Seagull Books, Calcutta.

Singh, S. (1987), *Scheduled Castes in India: Demension of Social Change*; Gyan Publishing, New Delhi.

Singhi, N.K. (1979), *Education and Social Change*; Rawat Publications, Jaipur.

Srivastav, S.P. (1982), *Educational Growth in India: Data Base*; NIEPA, New Delhi.

Steele, A. (1986), *The Hindu Castes: Their Law Religion and Custom*, Mittal Publications, Delhi.

Swaminathan, M.S. (1982), Educational Problems of the Scheduled Castes, Inaugural address, National Seminar on Educational Problems of the Scheduled Castes, Indian Institute of Education, Poona.

UGC, Facilities to Scheduled Castes and Scheduled Tribes in Universities and Colleges, A Report.

Varma, M. (1965), *An Introduction to Educational Research*; Mc Graw Hill Book Co.; Torento.

Y.D. Sharma, *Castes and Scheduled Tribes*; National Council for Educational Research and Training, New Delhi.

Yadav, S.K. (1983), *Harijan Awarness of Educational Schemes: Antecedents and Consequences*; Academics, Gurgaon.

Yadav, S.K. (1986), *Educational Schemes for Scheduled Castes*; Shree Publishing House, Delhi.

JOURNALS

"Eight-Fold Increase in Scheduled Castes Literacy", *Assam Information*, (27), 9-10 October-November, pp. 17-19.

Aggarwal, Y. (1987), "Some Aspects of Educational Development Among the Scheduled Caste Population in India", *Journal of Educational Planning and Administration*, 1(2). pp. 137-164.

Alexander, K.C. and *et al.* (1981), "Social Development of Weaker Section: A Study in Krishna District, Andhra Pradesh", *Behavioural Success and Rural Development,* 492), pp. 246-79.

Ammejan, M.S. (1984), "Background Variables of the Scheduled Caste and Tribe College Students", *Indian Education Review,* 19(2), pp. 28-36.

Amrik Singh (1990), "Mandal Commission: Educational Impact", *The Times of India,* 18.8.1990.

Azad, J.L. (1976), "Education of Scheduled Castes and Scheduled Tribes", *Journal of Indian Education,* 1(6), pp. 23-28.

Babu, Jeji, M. (1980), "Educational Progress of Scheduled Castes and Scheduled Tribes (1967-68 to 1977-78)", *EPA Bulletin,* October. (3), pp. 30-39.

Bose, N.K. (1970), "Scheduled Castes and Tribes: Their Present Conditions", *Man in India,* 50(3), pp. 319-49.

Chanda Sarkar (1976), "A Study of Stagnation in the field of Secondary Education Among the Scheduled Castes, Scheduled Tribes and Other Communities", *Bulletin of the Cultural Research Institute,* 12(1-2).

Chandolia, R.N. (1980), "Enrollment of Scheduled Castes in Educational Institutions", *Yojana,* 24(19), pp. 25-6.

Chaturvedi, A.R. (1986), "Harijans Students of Uttar Pradesh", *Social Welfare,* 33(1), pp. 30-31.

Chauhan, B.R. and Narayana, G. (1976), "Problem of Education Among Scheduled Castes Students in Uttar Pradesh", *Social Change,* 6(1/2), pp. 13-17.

Chauhan, B.R. (1969), "Scheduled Castes and Scheduled Tribes", *Economic and Political Weekly,* 4(4), pp. 257-63.

Chitnis, S. (1972), "Education for Equality: Case of Scheduled Caste in Higher Education", *Economic and Political Weekly,* 7 August, pp. 1675-81.

Chitnis, S. (1975), "Education of the Scheduled Castes", *Journal of Higher Education,* 1(2), pp. 167-78.

Choudhari, S.K. (1970), "Educational Progress in Rural Bengal: A Study of Four Villages", *Economic and Political Weekly,* 5 February, pp. 301-306.

Felice, SR. A. (1977), "Status of Harijan Students in Colleges", *The Indian Journal of Social Work,* 38(1), pp. 15-25.

Gour, J.S. and *et al.* (1989), "Values and Career Maturity of Scheduled and Non-Scheduled Caste High School Boys", *Indian Educational Review,* 24(2), pp. 115-119.

Jain, L.C. (1981), "Emancipation of Scheduled Castes and Scheduled tribes: Some Suggestions", *Economic and Political Weekly,* 16(9), pp. 325-332.

Kamat, A.R. (1981), "Education and Social Change Amongst the Scheduled Caste and Scheduled Tribes", *Economic and Political Weekly,* 14(31), pp. 1279-84.

Katyal, A. (1989), "UGC Plan for Scheduled Castes and Scheduled Tribes", *The Times of India,* 3 April, p. 3.

Khurana, G. (1980), "Educational Facilities for Scheduled Castes", *The Education Quarterly,* 31(384), pp. 31-35.

Nagaranjan, N. (1994), "Literacy Status of Scheduled Castes in Tamil Nadu: Some Issues", *Educational Review,* 100(8), pp. 121-24.

Nandu R. (1986), "Socio-Structural Variants and Higher Education Among the Scheduled Castes and Scheduled Tribes", *Social Action,* 36(2), pp. 166-82.

Pal, N.K. (1976), "An Assessment of Progress of Post-Matric Education Among the Scheduled Castes and Scheduled Tribes of West Bengal", *Bulletin of the Cultural Research Institute,* 12(1-2).

Pandey, B. (1986), "Educational Development Among Scheduled Castes", *Social Scientist,* 14(2-3), pp. 59-68.

Premi, K.K. (1984), "Educational Equality and Economic Opportunities: A Comparative Study of Scheduled Castes and Non-Scheduled Castes", *Journal of Higher Education,* 9 (Spring), pp. 363-73.

Premi, K.K. (1989), "Education of Disadvantaged Children: Issues in Universalisation of Elementary Education in India", *Perspective in Education,* 5(1), pp. 13-21.

Rajput, J.S. (1993), "Education: Focus on Weaker Sections, *Times of India,* 16.1.1993.

Ravindranath, M.N. (1981), "Educational Problems of Scheduled Castes", *Educational Review,* 87(4), pp. 69.74.

Roy Burman, H.K. (1956), "a Note on the Scheduled Castes and Scheduled Tribes of West Bengal", *Vanyajati,* 4(2), pp. 66-67.

Roy Choudhary, B.K. (1963), "Comparative Study of the Progress of Secondary Education among the Scheduled Castes and Scheduled Tribes of West Bengal", *Bulletin of the Cultural Research Institute,* Calcutta, 2(1), pp. 110-52.

Roy Choudhary, B.K. (1966), "A Note on the progress of Secondary Education Among Scheduled Castes and Scheduled Tribes of West Bengal", *Bulletin of the Cultural Research Institute,* Calcutta, 5(162), pp. 59-66.

Roy Chowdhary, B.K. (1964), Comparative Study of the progress of Secondary Education among the Scheduled Castes and Scheduled Tribes of West Bengal; *Bulletin of the Cultural Research Institute*, Vol. 3, No. 1; pp. 40-52.

Saha, R. (1978), "An Assessment of Progress of Secondary Education Amongst the Scheduled Castes and Scheduled Tribes of West Bengal during 1961-71", *Bulletin of the Cultural Research Institute,* Calcutta, 13(1-2).

Satyanarayana, B.S. (1982), "Educational Problems of Scheduled Castes College Students in Karnataka", *Journal of Higher Education,* 7(3), pp. 253-60.

Sharma, K.L. (1972), "Educational Problems of Scheduled Castes in Rajasthan", *Tribe,* 9(1-2).

Sharma, K.L. (1974), "Educational Inequalities Among Rajasthan's Scheduled Castes", *Economic and Political Weekly,* 9(37), pp. 1589-1592.

Shyam, L. (1970), Educational Development Among Bhangis in Jodhpur", *Tribe,* 7(1), pp. 26-31.

Singh, M. (1981), "How Equal are the Scheduled Castes?: Some Aspects of Their Educational Development", *Bulletin of the Cultural Research Institute,* Calcutta, 11, p. 85.

Swaminathan, M.S. (1982), Educational Development of the Scheduled Castes", *Journal of Indian Education,* 8(1), pp. 40-45.

Thiagarajan, A.P. (1987), "Educational Progress of Scheduled Castes", *Experiments in education,* 15(5), pp. 94-9.

Yadav, S.K. (1979), "Education of Scheduled Castes: Problems and Solutions", *Avaghana,* 3(1).

Yadav, S.K. (1979), "Intelligence, Motivational Tendencies of Scheduled Castes and Non-Scheduled Castes Secondary Students", *Journal of Education and Psychology,* 37(2), pp. 83-89.

Yadav, S.K. (1983), "Research Review on Implementation of the Educational Schemes of Scheduled Castes", *Indian Educational Review,* 18(3), pp. 112-22.

Zachariah, M. (1972), "Positive Discrimination in Education for India's Scheduled Castes: A Review of the Problem 1950-1970", *Comparative Education Review,* 16(1), pp. 16-29.